Outreach

Outreach

LIBRARY SERVICES FOR
THE INSTITUTIONALISED, THE ELDERLY,
AND THE PHYSICALLY HANDICAPPED

Gerald Bramley
FLA

CLIVE BINGLEY
LONDON

LINNET BOOKS
HAMDEN · CONN

FIRST PUBLISHED 1978 BY CLIVE BINGLEY LTD
16 PEMBRIDGE ROAD LONDON W11 UK
SIMULTANEOUSLY PUBLISHED IN THE USA BY LINNET BOOKS
AN IMPRINT OF THE SHOE STRING PRESS INC
995 SHERMAN AVENUE HAMDEN CONNECTICUT 06514
SET IN 12 ON 13 POINT ALDINE ROMAN BY ALLSET
PRINTED AND BOUND IN THE UK BY
REDWOOD BURN LTD TROWBRIDGE AND ESHER
COPYRIGHT © GERALD BRAMLEY 1978
ALL RIGHTS RESERVED
BINGLEY ISBN: 0-85157-254-5
LINNET ISBN: 0-208-01663-5

Library of Congress Cataloging in Publication Data

Bramley, Gerald.
  Outreach.
  Bibliography: p.
  1. Libraries and the physically handicapped.
  2. Libraries and the aged.   3. Hospital
libraries.   4. Prison libraries.   I. Title.   [DNLM:
  1. Libraries, Hospital.   2. Prisons.   3. Library
services.   4. Aged.   5. Handicapped.   Z711.92.H3
  B815o]
  Z711.92.P5B72   027.6   78-7281
ISBN 0-208-01663-5

CONTENTS

PREFACE

ONE IMPORTANT ASPECT of public library development in industrialised countries has been the introduction of services for the physically handicapped and the institutionalised. This has, largely, been a twentieth century phenomenon and one of the objectives of this work is to examine the social and economic factors which have contributed to the emergence of library provision for the disadvantaged.

The approach to the topics discussed has been partly historic, in order to indicate the slow evolution of the philosophy that the public library has a duty to reach out to those who are confined to their homes or an institution. This approach also demonstrates the growing acceptance by librarians that all members of society have a right to receive an adequate library service whatever their circumstances.

There are certain themes which run through each of the following chapters. It is apparent that the supply of reading material to the housebound, the disabled and the institutionalised has, in the past, depended heavily upon the willingness of volunteers to undertake the task of distributing books to those who need them. Indeed the presence of volunteers is still evident in the work of meeting the needs of the disadvantaged reader. This has meant that the quality of library services to the physically handicapped and those in hospitals and prisons has not reached that available to the rest of the community.

The changes which are apparent in the provision of books to the disadvantaged have stemmed, in part, from the greater

7

willingness of public libraries to recognise the special requirements of the disabled and the institutionalised. Another
contributory factor has been the availability of central
government grants to finance the development of library
services to the disadvantaged. This has been more apparent
in the United States than in Britain for example, and an
attempt has been made to show the impact which federal aid
has had upon library provision to the physically, visually and
mentally handicapped.

The book is designed primarily for students of librarianship and for those who are just beginning their professional
careers. There has, therefore, been an emphasis upon the
practicalities of organising and administering libraries in
institutions and on the methods for supplying reading material to the housebound and the disabled.

Some limitations have had to be observed in the examples
given of existing services, and the work is largely confined to
British and American experience. While there is more pro-
minence given to the provision of library facilities for the
disadvantaged adult, certain aspects of library work with the
sick and disabled child have been discussed. The bibliographical items cited are drawn predominately from Anglo-
American sources with the availability of books and articles
being a determining factor in selection.

ONE

HOSPITAL LIBRARIES:
the historical background

The United Kingdom
THE SYSTEMATIC PROVISION of reading material to patients in hospitals is largely a twentieth century phenomenon. There had been earlier, sporadic attempts to give the inmates of hospitals access to books, but this material was almost invariably of a devotional nature supplied by religious organisations. Conceivably the hope was that those in the extremes of suffering would welcome the solace that these uplifting tracts could bring.

Towards the end of the nineteenth century, there was some show of interest by the British library profession in the desirability of establishing collections of literature for hospital patients. The delegates to the Library Association annual conference of 1895 received a report on a survey which had been made of existing hospital library services.[1] This investigation had been conducted by Miss Dorothy Tylor. Seventy hospitals had been circulated asking for details of their book collections. The hospitals evinced little interest in Miss Tylor's questionnaire with only thirty-four making any return, the majority of these being institutions in London and the major urban centres. The findings of the survey were not therefore necessarily applicable to the entire country.

It was apparent that the standards of library provision did vary considerably from one hospital to another. One institution claimed to have a library of some seven thousand volumes, others had barely one hundred. One characteristic, common to every hospital, was that little or no attempt was

9

made to add new publications to the library as they were needed: ' . . . invariably we find that the library is provided and maintained by gifts of books, by subscriptions and donations from friends. . . '[2]

Miss Tylor also disclosed that although the majority of hospital medical staff favoured the supply of books to their patients, some doctors and nurses actively discouraged the provision of books to the inmates under their control. This lack of enthusiasm for the library service on the part of some members of the medical staffs was occasioned by the condition of the reading material being circulated in their wards. Many doctors were naturally worried that the dirt-encrusted volumes which formed much of the hospital library collections were potential sources of infection. The benefits that reading might bring to the sick were, in the doctors' opinion, outweighed by the dangers that the books might be transmitting disease.

The public library service in Britain was the natural agency for the supply of books to hospital patients. Unfortunately public libraries continued at this period to be hampered by the inadequate financial support which had dogged the public library service in Britain since its inception. Libraries could do little more than dispatch cast-off books and discarded newspapers and magazines to hospital patients.

There was a general awareness that a well-administered supply of books could do much to bring comfort and solace to the sick. Miss Tylor, in her address to the 1895 conference, summarised this feeling:

> I have been privately informed by nurses of experience, of the beneficial effects of reading upon patients—how it prevents them from brooding over their illness, how it amuses and informs them, how glad many of them are of a 'read' the taste for good literature being constantly found; and I can imagine that among the convalescents the passing of monotonous hours is made less irksome and that it provides topics for talk and discussion.[3]

While it was apparent to both librarians and to the majority of doctors that books could contribute to the well-being of patients, it was, in the early years of the twentieth century, beyond the resources of public libraries and hospitals alike to make more than a token supply of books available. It was the outbreak of the First World War that was to provide the necessary catalyst to the developments of libraries in hospitals. The crusading zeal of young men as they pressed into the recruiting offices, was echoed by young women as they worked with equal fervour to develop medical and other facilities for wounded servicemen. The provision of books to wounded soldiers and sailors was a natural part of this movement.

The first practical steps to establish library services for war-time hospitals were, largely, instigated by Mrs H M Gaskell. The story of the 'War Library' is already well documented[4] and it is sufficient to say that the growth of hospital libraries during the war profoundly influenced later developments. The most notable feature of war-time hospital library work was the active involvement of voluntary organisations, with the responsibility for the running of the War Library being quickly assumed by a joint committee of the Order of St John and the Red Cross.

The end of the war saw the St John and Red Cross Library extend its services gradually to civilian hospitals. This meant effectively that hospital librarianship, as it developed in the United Kingdom, was to be heavily dependent upon voluntary help and voluntary contributions. It ensured that the distribution of books to hospital patients would be in the hands of unpaid and untrained workers. It also meant that the reading material available for the sick would consist largely of donated books and out-of-date magazines. The participation of the public library service in the provision of hospital libraries was minimal. Kent and Durham County Library services, with a few other authorities, were honourable exceptions to this failure. The majority of public libraries were unable, or unwilling, to do more than send the occasional consignment of cast-off books to the nearest hospital.

The principal agent for supplying library facilities in hospitals was to be the St John and Red Cross Hospital Library, which developed from the war-time organisation. There were a number of other voluntary bodies which collected and distributed books to hospitals. These books had usually been donated by private individuals and would be taken around the hospital wards by the voluntary workers. One body which was prominent in this activity was Toc H which had been formed by 'Tubby' Clayton.

This reliance upon voluntary effort, coupled with the contribution of a pitifully small number of public libraries, was to be the totality of hospital library provision in Britain in the years between the two world wars. The work of the voluntary bodies was hampered by a chronic lack of assured and continuing financial support. Public libraries were equally prevented by inadequate resources from making more than a token contribution to the supply of books to hospitals.

Librarians at their professional gatherings discussed earnestly the plight of hospital patients. Delegates would vie with each other in condemning the deplorable state of library provision in hospitals. Their words would be received with solemn assent. Unfortunately little would be done to translate high-minded speeches into direct action.

The voluntary workers, and the very small number of professional librarians engaged in hospital librarianship, evidently despaired of any direct commitment by the Library Association to the cause of hospital library provision. In 1934 they formed the Guild of Hospital Librarians. The guild had two major initial accomplishments. The first was to introduce an effective system for training voluntary workers in the basic techniques of hospital library work. The second was to publish a journal, *The book trolley*, in which the techniques of hospital librarianship could be discussed and analysed.

The real advance of the public library service in Britain into the field of hospital library provision was not to come until the end of the Second World War.

The United States

The pattern of hospital library development in the United States was not dissimilar to that in the United Kingdom. Again, little progress was made until the outbreak of the First World War. 'Before the war, the number of organised libraries in hospitals and sanatoria might have been counted on the fingers of one hand. Books they had, gifts, discards from attics, old bound magazines, usually covered with brown paper and hidden away in linen closets or store-rooms . . .'[5]

With the outbreak of war came the first real beginnings of hospital libraries in the United States. There was, from the outset, one fundamental difference between the course of events in Britain and the United States. This was the early involvement of the American library profession through the work of the American Library Association (ALA).

The ALA's War Service was the equivalent of the British War Library, although the American operation was much larger. It was the main agency for organising supplies of reading material to servicemen who had been wounded. By the end of the war one hundred and fifty volunteers were working with the War Service, supplying books to servicemen in the United States and in France.[6]

The cessation of hostilities did not bring an end to the ALA's concern with the provision of libraries for hospitals. Immediately after the armistice, the association was organising consignments of books to those war-wounded who were being cared for in the US Public Health Service Hospitals for disabled ex-servicemen. As a further demonstration of its continuing interest in hospital librarianship, the ALA established its first Hospital Library Committee with a Hospital Library Round Table being formed at a later date.

By the late 1930s those librarians closely engaged in developing libraries in hospitals had begun to distinguish between the requirements of the library service for the professional staff and the more general service for the patients. The concept of duality was given support by the statement of objectives contained in the *National plan for libraries*. This

13

emphasised the dual nature of hospital librarianship and contained a suggestion that the larger hospitals should provide library services to both doctors and patients, with the medical and patients' libraries being administered either separately or as a single unit. Smaller hospitals, it was felt, could look to the public library for assistance in setting up libraries in hospitals, supplying them with reading lists and satisfying requests for specific books.

The variable quality of hospital libraries in Britain and the United States does emphasise the ambivalent attitude which professional librarians had towards the need to introduce adequate library services for the sick. The majority of public librarians were ready to acknowledge the value of books in hospitals, recognising the benefits which reading as an activity could bring to patients. However, to provide properly organised hospital library services would have required the diversion of resources from other sectors of the public libraries' responsibilities. Librarians clearly regarded hospital library work as a relatively minor priority, an area of librarianship which had closer affinities with social work than with librarianship. Hospital patients could, therefore, be safely left to the ministrations of voluntary workers who were better suited to meet the limited reading needs of the sick.

It was argued earlier that the close association of voluntary organisations with hospital library development, particulalrly in Britain, was far from beneficial. It provided British librarians with an excuse to delay the introduction of publically supported hospital library services. Equally, hospital administrators and doctors were often prepared to accept that the distribution of books to their patients was something which could and should be undertaken by volunteers. Indeed some members of the medical profession were openly hostile to the introduction of books into their wards.

In the face of apathy, and occasional antipathy, it is hardly surprising that there were few good hospital libraries in existence during the inter-war years. It needed more favourable economic and social conditions, and more awareness of the need to ensure that hospital patients who wanted access to an adequate supply of books should have this as of right.

Post-war developments

The outbreak of the Second World War saw a strengthening of the voluntary library services to both military and civilian hospitals. Some British public libraries also extended their facilities to hospitals and nursing homes for wounded servicemen. A potentially more significant factor in the evolution of hospital librarianship were the intensive discussions which took place in Britain during the war on the future of health care. The results of this dialogue were published in the Beveridge Report in 1942, with many of the report's recommendations later being embodied in the National Health Service Act which was passed in 1946 and came into operation in 1948. The act, in effect, nationalised the hospitals of the country, bringing them under the control of a minister of the crown.

It seemed to the Library Association and the Guild of Hospital Librarians that the creation of a unified national health service offered a tremendous opportunity to introduce a planned, nationally directed system of hospital libraries. The two bodies acted with commendable promptitude, and a joint deputation called on the newly created Ministry of Health armed with a memorandum which contained a number of proposals for developing a network of hospital libraries in the United Kingdom. The basic suggestions were as follows:

a) Responsibility for the provision of books and library staff in hospitals to rest primarily with the public libraries, with appropriate assistance from voluntary organisations already working in the field.

b) Each hospital regional headquarters to have a qualified librarian attached as a professional adviser.

c) Ultimately, all larger hospitals to provide a comprehensive library service, under the control of a professionally qualified librarian.

The deputation had hoped that the ministry would not only accept its proposals, but would also agree that the main costs would be borne by the health service. The officials who received the deputation quickly dispelled any illusions that these proposals had any prospect of being accepted in the immediate future. The National Health Service was hopelessly underfinanced from the outset.. The country was still attempting to recover from the effects of six years of war, and the resources which it could allocate to health care were strictly limited. In addition, the hospitals which the National Health Service has inherited were part of a ramshackle system which had its genesis in the Poor Law Regulations passed the previous century. In some cases the hospitals had been under the control of local authorities whose financial contributions had not always been sufficient to maintain an efficient service. Other hospitals were provided by charitable bodies from legacies, donations and collections. To weld this legacy into a viable and efficient health care structure would obviously tax the resources of the country, and in these circumstances the provision of reading material to patients was seen as a matter of marginal significance.

There was, already, an acceptable alternative: the St John and Red Cross Library had loyally supplied hospital patients with books throughout the war years. However, the society was now in financial difficulty, and had informed the Ministry of Health that it was unable to continue its services free of charge. The ministry offered to pay the society for its services at the rate of five shillings per head for each occupied bed in the hospitals which received its services, and further agreed to reimburse the salaries of those members of staff who were engaged as paid officials. Furthermore, the ministry also accepted the society's demand that where it was supplying a library service to a hospital it would be recognised as the sole agent. This effectively prevented any agreement between a public library and the St John and Red Cross Library to give a joint library service. The decision to favour the continuation of the St John and Red Cross Library in hospitals meant that, for the immediate future, voluntary agencies would be the predominant supplier of books to patients.

The Library Association fought bravely to secure the same financial assistance for public libraries which were willing to provide books and other assistance. It was suggested that public libraries could offer a service which would be at least comparable, if not superior, to that given by the St John and Red Cross. Public libraries could not only supply books, but would have the additional benefit of being able to draw upon the expertise of professionals. As part of its campaign, the LA issued a circular, exhorting public libraries to offer their services to hospitals in their area. The response to this call to action was muted. There were some practical difficulties, the most fundamental being the differing boundaries of the National Health Service and those of local government areas. There were few instances where the areas of responsibility of hospital management committees and local authorities exactly coincided, and in practical terms this could mean that a hospital which might logically be served by a nearby public library would, in fact, be situated within the boundaries of another local authority. A hospital area management committee, with several institutions under its control, might, theoretically, be required to negotiate with several public libraries in order to secure a supply of books to each hospital.

Another central and unsolved problem was the question of finance. If public libraries were to be actively involved in the provision of reading material to hospitals, who was to pay for this service? The LA, mindful of the agreement between the Ministry of Health and the St John and Red Cross, had suggested to libraries that the yearly cost of supplying books to a hospital would be between £1 and £1/10/0 per occupied bed. Of this the hospital might reasonably be expected to contribute five shillings, an amount which neatly coincided with the sum which the ministry had agreed to pay the Red Cross and St John. This was not, apparently, a view shared by the Ministry of Health. In 1951, it issued a statement stating that it had been advised that a local authority had no power to levy a charge for providing a library service to any hospital within its area. Although this statement was later withdrawn, it is reasonable to suppose that a number of public libraries were deterred from extending their services to local hospitals while the question of financial accountability was unresolved.

It seems, in the event, that there were a number of public libraries in the United Kingdom which were willing to brave the possible financial difficulties of offering a supply of books to hospitals. A survey conducted by the Library Association in 1957 was able to identify 173 public libraries which were giving hospitals some form of library service. The range of services being given and the financial arrangements which local authorities and hospitals had agreed upon were extremely varied. In some areas the library was meeting the entire cost of providing a service, sometimes the hospital would be supplying the necessary fittings and equipment, whilst the library provided the book stock and, perhaps, some professional assistance and advice. Generally, it seems that the quality of the service being given to hospitals by public libraries was not high, and indeed many libraries were not offering facilities of any kind.[7] A pilot survey of libraries in the North London area conducted in 1959, found that only four out of twenty-five library authorities made any sort of provision for hospitals.[8] Accompanying this survey were a number of recommendations for the future development of hospital libraries, including proposed standards for book provision.

It was apparent that little attention was paid to these and other suggestions for improving the quality of hospital library services. Another survey, conducted three years later, revealed that virtually no advance had been made beyond token contributions. The survey revealed that only one-third of the 278 library authorities in municipal areas could claim that they were giving even a minimum supply of books to hospitals within their localities.[9]

The legal and financial problems which had been partly responsible for the slow development of public library-

18

assisted services in hospitals were partly removed by the passing of the 1964 Public Libraries Act which covered England and Wales. The act required public libraries to co-operate ' . . . with any other authority whose functions are exercisable within the library area.' A number of public libraries interpreted this clause as a legal basis for cooperating with hospitals for the provision of books to patients. The act also defined those cases where a library authority would be entitled to levy a charge for services: ' . . . no charge shall be made by a library authority (otherwise than to another library authority) for library facilities made available by the authority.' This was regarded as authority for public libraries to levy a charge upon such institutions as hospitals which were receiving a specific library service.

This last assumption was briefly challenged, perhaps with some justification, by the Ministry of Health, but it is now generally accepted that a public library in England and Wales can, if it so wishes, charge for any or all of the services it provides to other organisations and institutions. This has not, however, led to any common pattern emerging in the fiscal arrangements which are made between public libraries and health authorities for the supply of books and other assistance to hospitals. Some public libraries have taken complete responsibility for the maintenance of book collections in the hospitals in their area; elsewhere the hospital authority has accepted responsibility for the entire costs, with the public library acting as an agency for the supply of the necessary staff, books and support services.

Summary
The most noticeable feature of hospital library development in postwar Britain has been the widespread acceptance by public libraries that they have a responsibility to reach those who are confined in hospital. This is by no means a universal acceptance of an obligation to provide an effective supply of books. The standard of service given by some public libraries to hospitals is still abysmally low. Many hospitals still rely upon voluntary organisations to supply their inmates

with reading material. However, the Library Association, through its Hospital Libraries and Handicapped Readers Group, has done much to encourage the development of properly administered hospital libraries for patients. The group, which was formed in 1962, in effect replaced the Guild of Hospital Librarians which was disbanded in 1953. Hospital librarians have been able to use the group to further the development of hospital library practice. Standards have been published to guide the formation of new hospital libraries, and provide guidelines for the development of existing patient library services. The group adopted the title of its predecessor's publication, *The book trolley*, for its own quarterly journal, now changed to *Health and welfare libraries quarterly*.

Perhaps the most significant development since the end of the Second World War has been the gradual recognition by British public libraries that they have a duty to serve their readers when they are confined to hospital. An extension of this would be to provide a library service comparable to that given by the average public library. This has been a standard which has proved difficult to achieve, and the reasons for this will be discussed in the next chapter.

REFERENCES
1 Tylor, Dorothy 'Hospital libraries' *The library* 7(83) November 1895, 347-352.
2 Ibid 348.
3 Ibid 349.
4 Sturt, Ronald 'Hospital libraries in Engand and Wales—a history' in *Hospital libraries and work with the disabled* (ed) Mona Going, Library Association, 1973, 26-29.
5 Jones, Edith Kathleen (ed) *The hospital library* Chicago, Ameri-London, LA, 1973, 26-29.
5 Jones, Edith Kathleen (ed) *The hospital library* Chicago, American Library Association, 1923, 1.
6 Ibid 4-9.
7 Cited by Pemberton, J E 'The role of public library authorities in the development of hospital library services' *Journal of librarianship* 3(2) April 1971, 106-107.
8 King Edward's Hospital Fund for London *Hospital library services: a pilot survey* London, the Fund, 1959.
9 Pemberton op cit 107-108.

TWO

HOSPITAL LIBRARIES:
organisation and administration

Patterns of provision
IN MANY COUNTRIES the principal agencies for the
provision of library services to hospital patients are voluntary organisations. The contribution of the St John and Red
Cross Library in the United Kingdom has already been discussed. In other parts of the world the Red Cross is equally
active in bringing books to those who are sick.

The Australian Red Cross is frequently the body to which
public hospitals in Australia look to for library provision. In
Belgium, the Conseil National Bibliothèques d'Hôpitaux de la
Croix Rouge (CNBH) is the most important national body
for supplying library facilities.[1] Another voluntary body in
Belgium, the Fédération des Institutions hôpitalières, plays
a valuable part in bringing books to the hospital patient.
This organisation is administered and financed by the Curitas
Catholica. Ten institutions in French-speaking Belgium and
forty five in the Flemish areas are served by this organisa-
tion.[2]

A 1971 survey of hospital library provision in New Zealand has been recently brought up-to-date by the New
Zealand Library Association Hospital Library Service Committee. The new investigation reveals that only twenty-nine
of the sixty-seven hospitals covered by the survey had their
bookstocks supplemented by public agencies. The remainder
were primarily dependent upon voluntary bodies for a
supply of books. These voluntary organisations include the
Red Cross, Hospital Auxiliaries and the National Council of
Women.[3]

Another common pattern of hospital library development
is for the public library service to undertake the major

21

responsibility for the provision of reading material to hospital patients. In certain of the Scandinavian countries and in some socialist states in Europe, the precise role of the public library in supplying a service to hospital patients is defined by law. Hospital libraries are, in effect, integrated into the national network of libraries.

A further possibility for the provision of library facilities in hospitals is for the central government to assume this as an obligation. An example of state participation in the supply of hospital library services is provided by the US Veterans' Administration (VA). This federal agency was founded to administer all central government benefits for ex-servicemen. Hospital, medical and health care benefits are administered by the Department of Medicine and Surgery of the Veterans' Administration. The VA hospital library network is highly developed embracing services to patients, medical, para-medical and administrative staff. The Veterans' Administration is financed as an independent agency by the US federal government.

Financial provision

The methods for determining responsibility for the costs of hospital library provision again vary from country to country. Where a voluntary organisation is the primary agency for supplying a hospital with a supply of books, a common practice is to levy a charge based upon the number of patients to be served in the institution. Another form of financial arrangement is for the central government to make annual grants to voluntary organisations which are willing to undertake responsibility for hospital library services.

In the United Kingdom the St John and Red Cross Society Library levies a charge per occupied bed. In Belgium the CNBH receives an initial payment to cover the library installation costs with an annual subsidy to meet running expenses.

When public libraries operate as agencies for the supply of reading material to hospital patients, there are a number of possible arrangements for determining financial accountability.

One possibility is for the public library to take complete responsibility for the provision of a library service to hospital patients. This is a system which operates in many areas in Denmark. Often, when public libraries have accepted the principle that they have a duty to those in hospital, the hospital becomes for library purposes a branch of the public library system. The hospital library will offer the same range of services and reading materials which can be found in small branch libraries operated by public libraries.

The cost of maintaining hospital libraries at this standard is considerable. The limited resources of public libraries in the United Kingdom does require that the relative importance of different branches of the service has to be established, and the development of hospital libraries is accorded low priority by the majority of British librarians. If a hospital asks the local public library to supply books to patients, the probability is that the public library will require the hospital to make some financial contribution to the costs of such provision.

Library services may be supplied on a contractual basis in which the precise duties and commitments of both the hospital and the public library will be clearly defined. The financial arrangements for contracts of this kind will vary. Sometimes the public library will supply reading material without levying a charge, the hospital being expected to meet the salaries of the staff engaged in this work and also to cover the costs of furnishing, fitting and equipping the library accommodation. The running costs — heating, lighting and maintenance charges — will normally be met by the hospital. The methods of determining costs will vary. Some libraries favour the method used by voluntary organisations, whereby the cost of a library service is determined by the number of patients served. An alternative is for charges to be based on the number of books supplied each year.

There are distinct benefits for the hospital which can secure the aid of a public library for the supply of reading material.

The expertise of professionals will be available for the development of its library; new materials can be obtained through the book order department of the public library; titles difficult to obtain can be dealt with through the same system; in short, the entire resources of the public library will be available to meet requests made by patients for specific books.

If a hospital lacks the necessary funds to commission a public library to act as an agency for the supply of reading material, other arrangements can be made. The majority of public libraries are willing to despatch consignments of books to local hospitals, distribution being undertaken by voluntary workers recruited by the hospital administration. This does in fact represent the total commitment made by many public libraries in the United Kingdom to the hospitals in their area. It is, at best, a poor substitute for a properly administered, adequately financed library service.

The hospital library

The practice of hospital librarianship needs further definition. 'Hospital library' is a generic term which can be applied to a number of separate libraries intended to service different sections of the hospital community. In any hospital there can be several collections of literature: a patients' library and independent libraries for both doctors and nurses. To compound the difficulties of terminology, individual members of the hospital community can often be users of more than one library: doctors and nurses will often draw upon the patients' collection for books of general interest. Doctors may occasionally borrow items from the nurses' library; certain items in the doctors' medical collection will be of use to nurses pursuing advanced courses.

In an attempt to rationalise library provision for the different sections of the hospital community, the concept of the 'integrated library' has been introduced. The intention is for all collections of literature in a hospital to be under the supervision of one librarian. The *Standards for libraries in health care institutions*, devised by the ALA's Association of Hospital and Institution Libraries, recommends that all such libraries be centrally administered.[4] Similarly, the US Veterans' Administration manual advocates that one librarian should control and direct the medical and patients' library programmes.[5] The standards for hospital libraries introduced by the British Library Association in 1972 suggest that the hospital librarian should be the 'responsible agent' for all aspects of library service in a health care institution.[6]

This consensus of opinion has not prevented patient and medical libraries in many hospitals from being developed as administratively separate departments. Indeed the view of many medical librarians is that lay and professional libraries cannot be successfully administered as a joint service. The clientele and the types of material provided by the two are seen as so different, that no common ground can exist. Developments in medical librarianship in the last twenty years have further strengthened this stance. The phenomenal growth of health science literature has necessitated the introduction of new techniques for the organisation and dissemination of the results of medical research. There have been two principal innovations in the field of medical librarianship which have had a direct influence upon the development of libraries in hospitals. The first and perhaps the most far-reaching factor has been the introduction of computerised techniques to collect and disseminate health science information. The second important event has been the foundation of regional medical library networks.

In both of these new programmes, the most important initial advances were made in the United States. The introduction of computerised techniques for the organisation of medical literature came with the National Library of Medicine's Medical Analysis and Retrieval System (MEDLARS) which began operations in 1964. By 1971 the advances which had been made in computer technology enabled the National Library of Medicine to offer its users MEDLINE (MEDLARS–ON LINE). Since then other medical information services have been introduced including CATLINE and SERLINE.

It was again in the US that the concept of the regional medical library saw its first practical expression when, in 1967, the New England Regional Medical Library was established in Boston. Within a comparatively short space of time, ten other regional medical library networks had been introduced to link US medical libraries on a cooperative level.

There have been comparable advances in the United Kingdom although the growth of medical library networks in the UK has lagged behind transatlantic developments. The first MEDLARS centre was established by the British Library in 1964, and by 1977 the British Library was able to offer a MEDLINE service as part of the British Library Automated Information Service (BLAISE). The emergence of medical library networks has not received the same attention in Britain as in the United States. However a pioneer regional hospital medical library network has been formed: the Wessex Regional Library and Information Service links hospital libraries with the Southampton University Medical Library. In the Oxford region there is a similar scheme based upon the medical literature resources of the university's Radcliffe Camera. Sheffield and Birmingham hospital regions are considering the introduction of hospital medical library networks.

These improvements in the supply of medical information to doctors working in hospitals has brought the work of hospital medical libraries into close working association with other health science libraries. Patients' library services are considered by medical librarians as an aspect of general librarianship. In the UK, the Library Association's Medical Section has consistently claimed that there is a wide gulf between patient and hospital medical library practice, and that it is therefore impractical to jointly administer the two services. Medical librarians further insist that the complexities of health science librarianship require that a hospital medical librarian needs to be thoroughly familiar with the latest techniques available for the retrieval of clinical information. To have the additional responsibility of administering the library for patients would make it difficult for the hospital librarian to give a comprehensive and efficient information service to the professional staff. Equally the education, training and experience necessary to be an effective patients' librarian is unlikely to form part of the background of medical librarians.

The ideal solution, which is supported by the recommendations of both the US and UK Library Associations' specialist committees, is that there should be one librarian with overall control of both patient and medical collections, as well as a professional librarian directly responsible for each library in the hospital. It has to be acknowledged that this ideal is far from being realised in the United Kingdom, even in the larger health care institutions.

The administration of hospital medical libraries falls outside the scope of this work. The probability that a hospital librarian may have to administer both the patients' and the medical collections does, however, influence both the organisation of a hospital's library services and the recruitment of the professional staff for the library.

Standards and recruitment

There have, in recent years, been published a number of standards for hospital library practice which almost without exception advocate that professionally qualified or trained librarians should be appointed to administer hospital libraries. The Library Association's standards of 1972 state that a chartered librarian is 'essential' for the effective administration of a hospital library.[7] The American equivalent emphasises that the minimum qualifications of a hospital librarian should be a master's degree in library science, awarded by an accredited school of librarianship.[8]

This Anglo-American insistence on the value of a professionally qualified librarian is not shared by all national standards for libraries in health care institutions. In some

27

countries (West Germany and Sweden are examples), it is only required for the hospital librarian to be 'trained'.[9] Elsewhere standards for hospital libraries may only recommend that a qualified librarian be employed in the larger or more specialist health care institutions.

A high proportion of existing hospital library standards have been published by professional library associations. These are only recommendations and hospitals and public libraries alike can ignore such proposals. However, in the Scandinavian countries, it may be necessary to meet certain minimum standards in hospital library provision before library authorities qualify for state grants. These requirements can include an insistence that professionally qualified librarians are employed to organise the supply of books to patients. In some socialist countries there are ministerial decrees supporting the appointment of qualified or trained librarians in the larger hospitals.

To fulfil the demanding requirements of the post, the person recruited to a hospital library needs definite professional and personal qualities. The hospital librarian often works in professional isolation, and it is probable that there will only be one qualified librarian to serve the entire hospital community. The librarian will be unable to draw upon the advice and assistance of colleagues which is available to those working in public and academic libraries.

Librarians of hospitals will, therefore, need to possess a high degree of professional and personal independence in order to meet the demands made upon them. Preferably they should have gained experience in a more junior capacity in another hospital library, though in practice, many of those now engaged in the field have been recruited from other branches of library work. The public library sector has provided a useful training ground for those now specialising in hospital librarianship. Similarly, special and even academic libraries have supplied hospitals with their professional library staff.

Librarians recruited to hospital library work from public libraries may not find it too difficult to adjust to the requirements of patients. The reading tastes of those who are sick do not differ in any substantial degree from those who are well. If those with a public library background are also required to administer the medical collections, they may find that the demands made upon their professional knowledge and experience are more taxing. Those who have gained their library experience in an industrial concern, or learned society, will usually find their background enables them to adapt to the requirements of administering the medical collections. Conversely the special needs and reading interests of the patients may take them into unfamiliar realms of library practice.

When the public library has assumed complete responsibility for the administration of a hospital library there is the possibility of seconding a qualified member of staff to the post of hospital librarian. The person seconded may be transferred to the hospital for a fixed period of duty, or may assume the position in a semi-permanent capacity.

There are potential advantages in securing staff in this way. There will exist formal and informal links with the public library, and the hospital librarian can use these channels to borrow material to augment his own library's stock. It will often be possible to draw upon the administrative services which the public library can provide. And if the librarians are only seconded for a fixed period, they will not necessarily feel committed permanently to this specialised branch of librarianship.

Inevitably there will be difficulties. The librarian seconded from the public library may have to convince the hospital staff that he or she is wholly committed to the objectives of the institution. The question of divided loyalties might arise, with the hospital library being seen as an independent service and not an integral part of the hospital community.

Professional education

The development of courses in hospital librarianship has been neglected, particularly in the methods and techniques appropriate to patients' library provision. One possibility

29

is to make programmes of education in hospital librarianship available in schools of librarianship. These could be taken as optional or elective subjects as part of students' initial professional education. Another method is to make courses available for qualified librarians who are contemplating or who have begun a career in hospital library practice.

Full-time courses:

In 1964, the British Library Association, as part of its revised syllabus for professional qualification, introduced an optional examination paper in hospital library work. The majority of library schools in the UK which were, at that time, preparing students for the LA examinations, began to offer programmes in library work with the sick and the disabled.

The new syllabus also contained an optional paper in medical librarianship which included certain aspects of library practice which were relevant to the provision of literature in health care institutions. It was possible for students in British schools of librarianship to specialise in those branches of library work which would provide the theoretical background for employment in a hospital library.

Since 1964, library education in the UK has undergone a series of changes, and few library schools are now preparing students for the examinations of the Library Association. Instead, schools are devising their own syllabuses and there have been many changes in curriculum content. Some library schools no longer offer hospital library practice as an optional paper, but now hospital library work may be part of the core paper on library administration, or may be included in the study of other, related subjects. Loughborough School of Librarianship, for example, offers a paper on library services to the disadvantaged, in which library provision in health care institutions is considered.

The introduction by library schools of programmes in hospital and related branches of librarianship has had a number of direct and indirect benefits. It has created a cadre

30

of young librarians who are aware, through their professional studies, of the importance of ensuring that library provision is made for those sick in hospital. It has not necessarily meant that every student who has elected to take a course in hospital librarianship has intended to specialise in this field. Instead, there are now, in many British public libraries, members of the professional staff who are actively furthering the development of library facilities in hospitals, prisons and other institutions.

Part-time courses:

There will, naturally, be a number of young librarians whose interest is stimulated by the course they have taken in hospital library practice. Some of these have found posts in this area of librarianship. For them a constant need, as with all librarians, is for refresher courses which can enable them to update their knowledge of developments in their field of interest. There will also be a number of librarians who did not study hospital librarianship during their professional training who have taken posts as hospital librarians. They too will value the opportunity to attend workshops, courses and meetings which will augment their knowledge of hospital library practice.

The responsibility for meeting the further education needs of hospital librarians has been met, in part, by the special sections of the professional library associations. In the UK, the Hospital and Handicapped Readers Group of the Library Association has organised refresher courses, workshops and conferences. These meetings have enabled hospital librarians to continue and extend their professional knowledge; to hear experts in areas related to hospital librarianship and also to discuss common problems. The ALA's Association of Hospital and Institution Libraries, now the Health and Rehabilitative Library Services Division, fulfils a similar role in the United States. In both countries these groups frequently publish the results of their proceedings, thus creating a body of literature which will assist other librarians who are working in hospital libraries.

There are similar developments in other parts of the world. In Denmark the school of librarianship has for a number of years been actively concerned with the provision of educational opportunities for hospital librarians. In cooperation with the Hospital Group of the Danish Library Association, the school has introduced courses, usually of three months' duration, for hospital librarians.

It can be fairly claimed that there has been some progress in recent years in the provision of educational and training programmes for hospital librarians. In spite of this there has been little provision for those librarians who wish to specialise in hospital library work at a later stage in their professional careers. Those who do transfer to hospital library practice from some other field of librarianship are compelled to learn the techniques and requirements of their new post by trial and error. The schools of librarianship are the natural agencies for providing programmes which would extend the expertise of practising librarians, but currently there are few courses of this kind for potential hospital librarians.

There is, perhaps, some justification for library schools adopting this policy of non-provision. As yet the professional skills and techniques of library work with hospital patients remain to be defined. Much of hospital library practice is based upon experience and observation. There is a pressing need for this empirical approach to be codified for the benefit of young librarians who wish to enter the field. Indeed the whole question of the recruitment, education and training of hospital librarians needs to be rationalised.

Personal qualities and medical knowledge

Working with the sick and disabled can bring considerable pressures upon the staff of a health care institution. As part of the hospital community the librarian will also be subject to these stresses. In addition to the personal qualities which characterise a good librarian, there is a need for certain attributes to meet the demands which life in a hospital brings.

Many of these personal qualities are to be found in the best doctors and nurses. A sense of compassion, and the capacity to feel deep sympathy, tempered with the ability to maintain an ultimate stance of emotional detachment. In an institution where tragedy is commonplace, a librarian will need to ensure that his or her feelings are not allowed to cloud professional judgement.

The librarian in a hospital requires a passionate belief in the value of the service which they are giving. Perhaps this is true of all librarians, but the hospital librarian serving the patients will be taking books to people who, in some cases, may be unfamiliar or even hostile towards books and reading. A firm conviction is needed that reading, as an activity in itself, will be of benefit to those who are sick. This belief must be harnessed to an acceptance that patients should not be unduly persuaded to accept reading material from the book trolley, that books are, at best, only a palliative for those who are gravely ill, and that those patients who decline to accept a book are the best arbiters of their own needs.

The ability to keep the value of a library service in perspective is also necessary. The medical staff's evaluation of the library service may be lower than the librarian's assessment of its worth. On occasion, the presence of a book trolley in a hospital ward can be an irritant, particularly during times of crisis. The librarian will have to recognise that the supply of light reading material to the inmates of a ward will seem a trivial matter to doctors and nurses intent on saving life.

The hospital librarian who is concerned only with the provision of a service to patients is unlikely to require a detailed knowledge of medicine. However, some awareness of the diseases and disabilities more commonly treated in the hospital will be useful. Similarly a familiarity with the effect which certain drugs have upon patients' powers of concentration will be of value when assessing individual reading needs.

A superficial knowledge of medical practice may contain inherent dangers and librarians should recognise this; it is their knowledge of the practice of librarianship which is their

33

principal contribution to the hospital community. This proviso having been made, it is reasonable for the patients' librarian to familiarise him or herself with the effects of illness and medical treatment. This can be accomplished in part by observation, and also by reading the more general health care magazines.

If the library service for the patients is also jointly administered with the medical library of the hospital then the librarian will need a detailed knowledge of medical literature and medical information networks. If they are further involved in the provision of a library service to medical students and to doctors undertaking postgraduate work then a working knowledge of medicine is desirable. Should the hospital library be serving postgraduate students and research workers, there is a strong case for it to be administered separately from the patients' library.

A recent development in the United States, which has received some attention in Britain, is the concept of the 'clinical librarian'. At a number of American training hospitals, librarians have formed part of medical teams as they conduct ward rounds. The intention is that the librarian follows up any clinical problems which arise during the examination of patients, and then conducts a literature search of material relevant to the case.

In order to examine the possibilities of the experiment, a pilot programme has been introduced in Britain at Guy's Hospital. This follows a visit made by Jean Farmer to those health care institutions in the United States where clinical librarians are employed. She has recently described her experiences and this has attracted comment from both librarians and medical practitioners.[10] The British view would seem to be that the presence of a librarian during ward visits, as part of the medical team, would raise insuperable problems. It would seem that if the post of clinical librarian becomes an accepted feature in teaching hospitals, then those appointed will need considerable medical knowledge, as well as a close familiarity with the sources of medical information.[11,12]

Non-professional and voluntary staff

The larger hospital libraries will require clerical personnel to support the librarian. They will perform the routine work of the department: maintenance of clerical records, supervision of loan procedures, preparation of material for the library shelves, possibly the delivery of books to the wards. Non-professional staff to undertake this work can be recruited by the hospital. Alternatively, if the patient library is provided on an agency basis by a public library, then the contractual arrangements may include the supply of the necessary support staff. The arguments in support of these two alternatives are finely balanced. There is a possibility that few of the junior staff of the public library will accept the demanding circumstances of the hospital and there may be a shortage of volunteers willing to undertake this work. The non-professional staff drawn from the public library will need special training if they are to meet the special requirements of the service. They will, as part of their basic training, be instructed in the conduct of ward rounds; they will be familiarised with the requirements of hospital discipline.

Those hospitals which recruit their own non-professional staff make as a criterion of selection the unique nature of the work. Certainly, in the United Kingdom there is no common policy in the important area of selection for the non-professional posts in hospital patient libraries, and this is a neglected aspect of hospital librarianship.

The recruitment of voluntary staff for the delivery of books to hospital patients has a long and honoured past. Indeed the employment of voluntary workers in hospitals is still an accepted practice. Voluntary workers are making an honourable and much-valued contribution to the work of hospitals and other institutions. They undertake time-consuming routine work, thus enabling the professional staff of the hospital to concentrate upon patient care. Voluntary work also gives an opportunity to members of the community with a strong social conscience to help those who are sick or disabled.

35

Several benefits arise from using voluntary staff in the hospital library.

i) The volunteer will almost invariably be highly motivated. They frequently possess qualities of compassion and sympathy, characteristics which are invaluable when working with the ill.

ii) The hospital can establish links with the local community through the volunteers, who can act as advocates for the institution. In some cases voluntary organisations may be willing to instigate local fund-raising activities. This can provide the hospital library with the necessary resources to purchase equipment: book trolleys, page-turners for disabled readers or talking-book machines for the blind.

iii) The presence of volunteers can provide a useful corrective to the sometimes over-professional atmosphere of the hospital. The librarian, employed in a full-time capacity, may be seen by the patients as another member of the establishment. Volunteers who are engaged by the library service to conduct ward rounds, can provide the necessary air of informality which will encourage the patients to relax and discuss their reading interests. Moreover, voluntary staff, particularly if they are recruited locally, can act as intermediaries between the patient and the outside world. They are able to discuss local affairs and matters of common knowledge and experience. This again can be a means of securing the patients' confidence, so that they will come to regard the visit by the book trolley as a pleasurable occasion.

iv) It has been suggested that a volunteer has greater patience than full-time staff. They are willing to spend time with those who are unfamiliar with books, providing them with the necessary advice and assistance.

There are, then, tangible gains to be secured from the help which volunteers can give. It also must be recognised that there are certain limitations to the contribution which they can make, particularly in those hospital services which make heavy use of voluntary assistance. The volunteers will essentially be amateurs and this runs contrary to the trend of gradual introduction of professionally administered hospital libraries. It is difficult to provide the necessary training programmes for voluntary workers who, for the most part, can only devote a few hours each week to the hospital library.

An attendant problem is that the employment of volunteers, even in an institution which has traditionally accepted unpaid assistance, may have the effect of lowering the status of the library. It is difficult to present the library as a fully professional service if the books are distributed to the patients by unpaid staff. The area in which the volunteer can be employed in the library is therefore restricted, and they can hardly be employed at all in the hospital medical library, except on the most routine tasks.

There may, too, be the occasional volunteer who is motivated less by a desire to help those who are ill, but rather by a morbid preoccupation with pain and death. However, the experience which hospitals have gained in the employment of voluntary help, will usually be sufficient to identify those with traits of this kind.

The ultimate factor to determine whether ot not volunteers will be employed is that of economics. The development of effective hospital library services has often been retarded by a lack of adequate financial support. It is sometimes the case that the employment of voluntary assistance is the only possible way in which a supply of books can be provided for the hospital patients. It has appeared logical to hospital administrators, when faced with a severe shortage of financial resources, to recruit those who are willing to work in the library without pay.

Whether voluntary assistance will continue to be available in the future is open to question. There has been a steady reduction in the number of people with the leisure to undertake voluntary work. Married women, who have traditionally formed the principal source of voluntary labour, are now often to be found in full-time employment in commerce and industry, and the trend towards professionally administered hospital libraries may be accelerated by social pressures of this kind.

The institution and the patient

The hospital as an institution possesses certain unique characteristics. If the patients' library is to play an effective part in the hospital community, its staff will need to be aware of the complex nature of the administrative structure within which they are working. Perhaps more than any other institution, the hospital is concerned with the fundamental matters of life and death. While this primarily affects the medical staff, other members of the institution—administrators, typists, porters and librarians—will be conscious of the pressures which are part of the hospital environment. The need to avoid mistakes, which might have grave consequences, will impose a discipline which would be unacceptable in other organisations. The librarian will need to be constantly aware of, and rigidly observe, the code of behaviour which governs every individual in the hospital community. It is only by accepting the strict standards of hospital discipline that the library in a hospital will be accepted by the medical staff as an integral part of patient care.

It has been suggested that the hospital is an example of a theoretically impossible administrative unit. There will usually be three main strands of control: medical, nursing and administrative. The fields of responsibility will be delineated by custom, and no member of the administrative staff would contemplate intervening, except in extreme circumstances, between doctor and patient. The library staff will need to cooperate with all three streams of management, as well as the many ancillary workers which form part of the hospital community. These ancillary workers will include teachers, who work in childrens' wards, social workers and the hospital chaplain.

The apparently disparate elements which constitute the hospital community might give the impression that there is a lack of cohesion in the institution. In practice the different workers in a hospital are united by a common goal: the well-being of the patient. In order to restore patients to health it is necessary for the various groups in a hospital to work closely together, and the concept of 'teamwork' is constantly stressed by writers on hospital administration. The hospital librarian, while needing to be aware of the complex nature of the hospital community, will also need to recognise the essential unity of this organisation.

It was suggested in the previous chapter that the patients' library should be at least capable of offering a service comparable to that available in the average public branch library. One factor which makes this ideal difficult to achieve is the nature of the patient community in a hospital. The majority of those being treated will not be regular users of the public library; they will not habitually read books. Nevertheless, the hospital librarian must assume that all patients are *potentially* in need of a supply of reading material. The special circumstances of hospital life, with a long period of enforced inactivity, provide the conditions which will often persuade non-readers to accept a book if it is offered to them.

It could once be assumed that hospital patients were drawn predominantly from two age groups: the very old and the very young. Today the hospital patient community will include all age groups and all sections of society. While, in the past, disease did strike the old, the young and the poor disproportionately, now people of all ages and all social classes are at risk. Certain infectious illnesses which were prevalent thirty years ago and which particularly affected children have largely been eliminated. Some complaints which were once associated with old age are increasingly afflicting those in middle life, heart disease and cancer being two examples. And the likelihood of being involved in a road accident is a risk to which all sections of the community are exposed.

With this change in the characteristics of those admitted to hospital, the reading interests which must be provided for are likely to be as diverse as those encountered by the public library. There will be important differences, occasioned by the presence of a substantial number of patients whose normal reading does not extend beyond a daily newspaper or occasional magazine, or even more rarely a paperback.

When determining on the appropriate reading material, the hospital librarian will need to take into consideration the diverse nature of the community to be served. Paperbacks, newspapers and periodicals will, of course, be widely available in the wards, purchased by friends or relatives as visiting presents. This does not preclude such provision by the hospital library service. Light fiction will be an essential part of the stock of the hospital library, and some of the more popular novels should be in paperback as this will be a more familiar physical format for those who are not regular users of the public library.

Reading ability can often be affected by the illness or injury from which the patients are suffering. It may be difficult to hold or to concentrate upon a book. But the effects of illness or injury will be varied: those who are recovering from a minor operation will normally find little significant change in their reading habits. This will be equally true of those admitted for exploratory tests.

Other patients, in contrast, may be experiencing severe discomfort, or may be in constant pain. In these cases there will be little desire to read. Very often medical treatment can affect powers of concentration: certain drugs can induce drowsiness, others temporarily distort the vision. The librarian will need to be sensitive to the patient's condition and not press books upon those whose illness or treatment precludes reading anything more demanding than a newspaper. There is, however, a legitimate entitlement to gently persuade the non-reader to select a book from the library trolley, if it seems they might benefit from a light novel. The librarian must distinguish between the reading needs of the 'short-stay' and the 'long-stay' patient in planning the service. The short-stay patient:

For those confined to hospital for less than a fortnight (the majority of patients), the time spent away from normal affairs will not represent a serious interruption to their lives. The occasional appearance of the book trolley will be their only contact with the hospital library service. This visit will be seen by most inmates as an opportunity to borrow those books most suited to relieve the tedium of their surroundings. They will normally seek out those books which do not make any great demands upon their concentration, for the hustle of the average public ward in hospital will make serious reading difficult. In these circumstances, light fiction works can have great value, whatever their literary merits. If a popular novel can provide patients with the means to escape from their immediate problems, it fulfills an important purpose. If the book also gives the patient both pleasure and enjoyment, it will have contributed to recovery.

Even those who habitually read more serious material may welcome access to light reading. It would be wrong, however, to assume that even in a hospital of predominantly short-stay nursing, the library service will be restricted entirely to the distribution of light reading material. There will be a number of patients who are mentally alert, who regard the period while they are confined to bed as the opportunity to turn to books which they have been prevented from reading before. It will be a chance, too, perhaps, to extend reading habits through choosing books on unfamiliar subjects.

The patients' library in a short-stay hospital should attempt to anticipate requests for the more popular titles and subjects. The book-stock should contain a selection of light novels, including romances, westerns and mystery stories in both hard-back and paper-back format; the better-known 'classical' fiction titles; a choice of reputable fiction by modern authors; and a range of popular non-fiction.

There will, in practice, be few hospital libraries capable of meeting more than a small proportion of the requests for books by the patients. Even the patients' libraries in the larger hospitals will have to rely upon the assistance of other libraries for the loan of reading material. Certain requests can be anticipated, these can be identified by maintaining records of the requests made by patients on the ward rounds. The book selection can then be guided by the expressed demands of the patients.

The requests for titles or subjects not represented in the hospital library may be obtained from another agency, possibly a public library. The majority of public libraries will be willing to meet requests for specific titles or books on particular topics from hospitals in their locality. Few, however, will be able to supply the immediate service which the situation may require. In a short-stay hospital the probability is that the patient making the request will have left the hospital before the item can be supplied. In institutions of this kind the librarian will have to accept that the level of library service will be below that given by the average public library. It will be primarily restricted to supplying books which afford diversion, pleasure and entertainment. A service of this kind should not be discounted, for reading material of the most popular kind can contribute towards the patient's progress to recovery by acting as a distraction from the difficulties of the present.

The long-stay patient:

In those hospitals or wards where patients are undergoing prolonged treatment there may be a requirement for a more comprehensive library service. While some long-stay patients will be content with a supply of recreational reading material, others may benefit from access to a wider choice of books. The librarian will often need to distinguish between the reading interests of the elderly and the younger patient. Illness or serious injury can bring a sudden and traumatic disruption of a young person's life. For someone who has been leading a full and active life, confinement in a hospital will induce a feeling of severe frustration. However the young patient can, in most cases, anticipate partial or complete recovery. This is a prospect often denied to the older person, who sometimes may only be hoping for a peaceful end. The librarian's approach to widely different demands will be conditioned by this consideration.

The young patient:

There are several ways in which books and other reading materials can help the younger patient who is confined to hospital for a lengthy period:

i) They can have a therapeutic effect. Reading as an activity, as suggested earlier, can divert attention from illness or injury.

ii) Some young people will be attending courses at college or university, and the librarian can, in some cases, act as intermediary between the patient and the educational institution. It may be possible for the librarian to obtain the readings necessary for the student to continue with studies while in hospital.

iii) If the patient is undertaking a course of occupational therapy, the librarian can arrange to supply books and other material related to this work. This will only be done after consulting the therapist in charge of the case.

iv) When the patient is unlikely to be able to resume his or her former employment, the librarian can obtain appropriate career books to help in the choice of an alternative vocation. Again this will be done in association with social workers and therapists.

v) There are occasions when patients' disabilities incapacitate them from work of any kind. For those in this situation a supply of books and related materials can help to reinforce the reading habit, providing a valuable form of recreational activity. Books can be an introduction to suitable interests and activities. The librarian will select books which cover those leisure interests which will not require physical agility or strength. Books can be a means of developing a new hobby, learning a language or acquiring knowledge of fresh subjects.

When the patient finally leaves hospital, the librarian can notify the public library, giving details of the individual's areas of interest, so that the staff can anticipate requests in these subject fields.

The elderly patient:

The problems which confront the elderly who are confined in hospital for a lengthy period are different in nature and intensity from those which the younger patient encounters. Genontological complaints may necessitate prolonged hospital treatment and are often progressive and irreversible. Even so, books can provide an escape for the elderly from the monotony and, in some instances, hopelessness of their condition. For those with few visitors, books and other reading material can provide a link with the outside world. It can also be a means of reliving the past: often a source of considerable pleasure for the elderly (see pages 113-5).

There are problems which often arise when supplying the elderly with reading material. Some find it difficult to hold books, and there are a number of reading aids available to help those with physical disabilities.

A high proportion of those in geriatric wards will be suffering from sight defects of varying severity. This may range from complete blindness to an inability to read books printed in type of normal size. A collection of large-print books will be welcomed, and the library can also consider the possibility of providing magnification aids. For those who are completely blind the librarian can secure the loan of books in embossed type (see chapter seven), or, if there is sufficient demand, the hospital library can build up its own collection. Books recorded on tape (talking books) can also be obtained, and patients in London hospitals are eligible for the service established by the British Library of Tape Recordings (see pages 162-3).

Children in hospital

To be taken into hospital can be a daunting experience for an adult; for a child it can be a terrifying ordeal. The sudden parting from parents, a new and awesome environment, the close proximity of strangers are disturbing in themselves. When these factors are combined with an illness or sudden accident, they can produce a sense of profound disorientation and insecurity in even the most emotionally well-balanced child.

The library can help the child become adjusted to the new surroundings by supplying familiar reading material which lessens the sense of being cut off. The child may welcome the appearance of books read and enjoyed in health. Books of this kind will be greeted as old friends, providing a sense of continuity and a reassurance that the world outside still exists.

There may be some virtue in providing books with an uplifting message. If possible, books can be found with stories of children who have been unwell, who have successfully overcome their illness. Children may derive some comfort from books of this kind.

Some children in hospital will be unable to read, either because they are not of school age, or through unwillingness to try because of the effects of their illness or treatment. In those hospitals where parents are allowed to stay with their children, books suitable for reading aloud will be welcome.

Children who are confined to hospital for a lengthy period will often be able to continue their education. In the United Kingdom, since 1908 teachers have been appointed to give, as far as possible, a normal programme of education for children in hospital. Those children of pre-school age may have a nursery teacher to introduce educational and recreational activities. In some children's hospitals there may also be 'play therapists' who will be active in organising entertainment and events.

The hospital library will support the educational work of teachers and therapists where this is necessary. This may require the supply of basic textbooks, but more usually this material will be under the control of the teaching staff. Normally the educational role of the hospital library will be broadly similar to that of the children's department of a public library. It will supply books and other material which will supplement and extend the teaching which the child is receiving.

If there is a programme of recreational activities for the children, the hospital librarian may find that there is a demand for books to support this work. The library of the hospital can act as repository for non-book material which will supplement the recreational programmes. This might include audiovisual material and also toys, games and word cards.

In general hospitals which contain children's wards, the hospital library will normally supply the reading needs of young people through visits by a book trolley or by establishing deposit collections. The assumption in the general hospital must be that it is not practicable for children to visit the library, though this situation can vary in a paediatric hospital where there may be children who are physically capable of making their way to the library. Children who are ambulant can be brought in organised groups to the library for specially arranged activities. These can include storytelling, play readings, films and slide shows.

For children who are admitted to hospital for short periods, reading needs will usually be adequately served by ward collections consisting of popular books and periodicals. A collection of books should also be kept for mothers, teachers and play therapists in the hospital library. This collection will be used to supplement the ward collections. The hospital library should attempt to provide more than a token collection of children's reading material. While the library may be prevented from displaying all those books which may be needed by the children while they are in hospital, it should attempt to meet requests made by children, parents or teachers. This can be achieved by establishing the necessary arrangements with another library, usually the local public library.

There is a strong case for a librarian to be employed fulltime in the paediatric hospital. The person appointed would be trained in all aspects of library work with children, and would also be familiar with the specialist aspect of the post. This would include a knowledge of the effect of illness upon a child's reading ability, therapeutic activities with books to aid the convalescent child and some training in child psychology. As with so many aspects of hospital library provision the ideal is far from being realised, and this must be considered a thoroughly unsatisfactory condition. Until such time as qualified children's librarians are automatically appointed to paediatric hospitals, the significance of the contribution which the library can make to the life of the institution will be minimal. Eileen Cummings has proposed that there should be a librarian, based at the public library, with responsibility for children in hospitals and institutions within the area being served by the library.[13] Even such an unambitious suggestion has little possibility of being implemented in the United Kingdom in the foreseeable future.

The ideal service would see a full-time children's librarian in every paediatric hospital, with provision for children in general hospitals being supervised by a visiting children's librarian. It is paradoxical that at that time when the quality of library services to children has improved immeasurably in the past decade, the sick and hospitalised child still has so little provision made for reading needs.

Non-book material in the hospital library

In addition to supplying books and magazines, the hospital library may find it necessary to provide a collection of audio-visual material which might include gramophone records, tapes, slides and possibly films. This will require the acquisition of the necessary equipment, the cost of which could place a considerable strain upon the resources. It is possible for the hospital librarian to justify expenditure on audio-visual items if the library has an extension programme for ambulent patients. In long-stay hospitals gramophone records and other non-book material will be valuable if the library is concerned with therapeutic activities. Some hospital libraries do provide extensive programmes including record recitals, films, talks and discussion groups and those book centred activities which are embraced by the term bibliotherapy.

Censorship

The librarian providing a service to hospital patients is subject to certain constraints in the selection of books. There are particularly novels which deal with the subjects of illness and death in a morbid fashion, and the librarian may feel that patients who are seriously ill, who perhaps fear that they are suffering from a complaint which might prove fatal, should not be given works of a depressing nature. Books which dwell upon sickness and human mortality would hardly be suitable for patients who are gravely ill. This confronts the hospital librarian with a dilemma, for to reject all those books which contain passages in which sickness and death are described in vivid fashion would drastically reduce the choice of titles available to the patients.

The librarian clearly has to exercise common-sense. There are a few novels which could easily cause distress to patients suffering from certain illnesses, and Solzhenitsyn's *Cancer ward* would naturally not be taken into a ward in which the inmates were suffering from carcinoma. But the main concern must be to avoid banning books from hospital collections which could safely be offered to the majority of patients.

The public are aware that medical science has made considerable advances; but they are equally aware that the medical staff do, occasionally, make mistakes. The librarian who declines to add novels which emphasise the human frailty of doctors and nurses to the collection, is guilty of professional malpractice. The patients, in most cases, should be given the opportunity to exercise their own judgement in deciding upon the verasimilitude of such works. In genuine cases of doubt the librarian can refer books which might endanger the well-being of patients to the medical staff.

Education and counselling

Physicians have, until recently, taken the view that patients should not be given access to medical literature, and books containing information on an individual patient's complaint

48

would be regarded as unsuitable reading material for the person concerned. There has been some change of opinion in recent years and doctors now see patient counselling as an important part of their work. The general public is more sophisticated than in the past. Newspapers and magazines frequently contain articles discussing the latest advances in medical treatment. An equally wide range of medical information on health and health care is relayed by television.

Hospital patients, in consequence, are more insistent on being given information about their illness, the nature of the treatment they are receiving and the possibilities of cure. This information is not always forthcoming. The concept of patient education has not been accepted wholeheartedly by every member of the medical profession. Patients do often leave hospital without being informed of the results of tests, the restrictions which their ailment places upon their future lives, or the prospects for recovery.

Those medical practitioners who are advocates of the need for patient education stress the value of an atmosphere in which hospital patients are encouraged to ask questions on matters that are giving them concern. They feel that the doctors and nurses should answer such questions promptly, courteously and correctly. The philosophy is that effective communication between the medical staff and the hospital inmate will hasten the patient's recovery.

There are several possibilities for the hospital library to cooperate in programmes of patient education. Patients might welcome information on the nature of their new environment. A booklet could be prepared, in conjunction with the medical and administrative staff, containing information on the layout of the hospital, the names of the wards and the consultants in charge of the major departments, and also listing meal-times, visiting times, special facilities and services.

Once discharged, the patient needs to know, amongst other things, any restrictions imposed on physical exertion, dietary requirements and the advisability of smoking or drinking alcohol. Doctors may be prevented by lack of time from counselling patients as fully as they would like, and, the hospital library can help the patients in this, both while in hospital and when discharged. While the patient is being treated, access to a collection of medical literature, written in terms comprehensible to the lay person, could be of value in explaining the nature of their illness. Literature to be included in a collection of this kind would, naturally, have to be approved by the medical staff. The patients, it has been argued, will be aided in their recovery if they are given a planned programme of instruction on their physical condition and progress. There are a number of books, pamphlets and other publications, written by physicians for the general public, which could be acquired by the hospital library. Material of this kind is often to be found in the stock of public libraries. If the patient has found an item to be of use then the hospital librarian can refer the patient to the public library when they leave hospital. A further step would be to inform the public librarian of the probable visit by the patient.

Once the patient is discharged, his family will need to be informed of the individual's physical and mental state. The doctor may recommend a number of published items which provide information on medication, diet, exercise, rest and other factors which are relevant to recovery. The hospital librarian can act as intermediary between the patient's family and the local public library which may be able to supply this literature.

If the hospital library is to be involved in any programme of patient education it must be with the full approval of the medical staff. There will be occasions when the seriousness of the patient's condition or mental state will preclude giving anything but the most generalised information about the illness and the prospects for restoration to health. In such circumstances the librarian would not attempt to give the patient any literature on his or her complaint. In some hospitals the medical staff may be opposed to the patient being given access to health information. The librarian must accept this decision without question. If librarians are to be accepted as integral members of the professional hierarchy of the hospital they will have to accede to the discipline of the institution.

Ward services

In hospitals where the majority of patients are short-stay, the emphasis of the library service will be upon the delivery of books to the wards. There are two basic methods for carrying this out—by depositing collections of literature in each ward or by a system of ward rounds with the books being taken to the patients' bedsides.

Deposit collections will usually consist of small collections of books and periodicals situated in a convenient place in the wards. It will need to be kept up-to-date and in good physical condition if it is to be of any value to the inmates of the hospital. This presupposes that the collections will be changed frequently and on a regular schedule. This method does have marked limitations:

i) It is difficult to supervise the use of the ward collections and there will, inevitably, be a high loss-rate. In practice this will not be significant since the material deposited in the wards should consist prodominantly of ephemeral literature: light novels, paperbacks and magazines.

ii) There is frequently a shortage of space in public wards and the medical and nursing staff might object to the potential loss of space which a ward collection would represent.

iii) A high proportion of patients will be unable to leave their beds to use ward collections.

In consequence, the majority of hospital librarians consider the ward round to be the most effective method for bringing the library service to the patient. The books to be taken to the individual wards can be selected to meet the reading tastes of the majority of the patients, and the library staff member who accompanies the trolley will be able to assist patients in their choice of books.

There is a strong case for the ward rounds to be conducted by a professionally qualified member of the library staff. This will be the only contact which many readers will have with the library service. The patient will often require assistance and a qualified, experienced librarian will be the best person to give this. Unfortunately ward rounds are, in British hospitals, often conducted by a non-professional member of the library staff or a voluntary worker. This is the result of pressure on the time of the qualified staff. Indeed, regretably, in many hospitals there will not be a professional librarian working with the library service. In those cases where there is one, he or she should at least maintain a close supervision of the ward rounds. The book requests received from the patient should be examined and, as far as possible, satisfied. A regular accompaniment of the ward rounds helps the professional to assess the efficiency of the service and to consider what improvements might be made. It also enables the liaison with medical and nursing staff to ensure that the library rounds are harmonised with the routine of the wards.

The book trolley for the wards rounds will need to be carefully designed and constructed. It needs to be equipped with a work surface to enable staff to perform the necessary clerical routines—recording loans, noting requests and suggestions etc. The trolley should be sufficiently manoeuvrable to be wheeled easily into lifts, along corridors and in between beds and other obstructions. There are a number of different models available, including motorised book trolleys, which have the advantage of being able to carry a larger display. The motorised trolley is especially useful when the hospital is housed in several buildings and the books have to be transported over a large area.

The patients' library will act primarily as a bookstore in those hospitals where the emphasis is upon ward services. When the library is used extensively by the hospital staff and where there is a high proportion of ambulant patients, then the library will operate as a conventional service-point providing the same range of facilities as a small public library.

Library accommodation

In older hospitals, where a library service is being introduced for the first time, the librarian will have to accept such accommodation as may be available. This will not be the situation in a modern establishment, where the library has been planned as an integral part of the building and where, from the outset, the librarian has been able to formulate his requirements. He will be, first of all, anxious to secure the best possible site. It may be difficult to secure the ideal location, for the library service will not always be seen by the hospital administration as a vital part of the institution, but the librarian should resist attempts to relegate the library to an unsuitable part of the hospital complex. If it is to be an effective part of the life of the hospital, the library needs to be adequately accommodated and in a good position.

In advancing proposals for the best location for the patients' library the librarian should be guided by the following considerations:

i) The library should be situated as closely as possible to the majority of its potential users. This will, in effect, mean it being in close proximity to those wards with the largest number of ambulant patients.

ii) A proportion of those wishing to visit the hospital library will be in wheelchairs or on crutches, and it should be sited so that these patients will not have to negotiate stairs or steps. If the hospital building is multistoried, the library should be as near as possible to a passenger lift. This is also helpful for the library staff taking the book trolleys to the wards.

iii) The hospital library may be an integrated service, providing for all sections of the hospital community, and giving access to medical information as well as a supply of more general books and other material. If practicable the library should be as near as possible to those areas where the medical staff work and live.

iv) If the patients' library is receiving agency services from a public library, close proximity to a loading bay will be an advantage for the delivery and return of books.

v) If optimum conditions are possible, the library should be situated in a quiet part of the building. This could mean that it would not be near to the majority of its potential users, and as with other factors, this will have to be a matter of compromise. The librarian must be willing to accept a certain noise level in order to ensure that the library is in an acceptable position.

The library should be designed so as to give an impression of quiet, encouraging its users to browse through its collections. If it can achieve this atmosphere it will be a refuge and haven from the stresses of hospital life. The furniture and the fittings should be chosen to convey a feeling of comfort and welcome. The use of warm colours for decoration, with the floors well carpeted, should combine to give the visitor a sense of well-being, even contentment. This environment, in addition to attracting users, can also contribute to the patients' return to health.

The accommodation allocated to the library will be determined by the services it is expected to provide. It is also necessary to secure space for the administrative and routine work which is an essential part of the work of any library. A hospital library designed for the general reading needs of both staff and patients will require the following areas:

1 Shelf accommodation for the bookstock.

2 A reading area with tables, chairs and a periodicals display rack.

3 Circulation desk.

4 An activities room which will be necessary if the library has an extension programme for ambulant patients.

5 Reference area containing basic reference materials, bibliographical aids, library catalogue and enquiry desk.

6 Special collections: large print books, books in braille, talking books, audio-visual materials (tapes, slides, films).

7 Work-room/office containing shelves, work tables, chairs, filing cabinets, space for loading and unloading book trolleys for the ward rounds.

8 Staff accommodation: rest area, lockers, wash-room.

The library must of course be adapted to help the high proportion of users who will be suffering from some form of physical handicap. In addition to the patients who are compelled to use wheelchairs or crutches, there will be those who are recovering from an illness or operation. The librarian should ensure that there is sufficient seating accommodation available to meet the needs of the total number of readers likely to be present at any one time. Some of the chairs should be designed specifically for the physically handicapped. The hospital patients' library should, in general, provide an environment in which the elderly and the disabled can move with the minimum of inconvenience and discomfort.

REFERENCES

1 International Federation of Library Associations, Libraries in Hospitals Sub-Section *Organization and description of work and statistics of library services in hospitals, institutions and for the handicapped* The Hague, IFLA, 1977.

2 Ibid

3 Ibid

4 American Library Association, Association of Hospital and Institution Libraries: Hospital Libraries Committee *Standards for libraries in health care institutions* Chicago, ALA, 1970, 3.

5 US Veterans' Administration, Department of Medicine m7, chapter 17. *Library service* Jan 22, 1969. Washington, DC, Veterans' Administration 1966-1969, 17.04.

6 Library Association *Hospital libraries: recommended standards for libraries in hospitals* London, LA, 1972, 5.

7 Ibid, 5.

8 ALA, Association of Hospital and Institution Libraries op cit

9 IFLA op cit

10 Farmer, Jean 'Medical libraries in the patient care setting' *Library Association record* 79(2) February, 1977, 81-85.

11 Manwaring, Leonard 'Should librarians invade patients' privacy? *Library Association record* 79(4) April, 1977, 221.

12 Wade, Jenny 'Ethics of clinical involvement' *Library Association record* 79(6) June, 1977, 329.

13 Cumming, Eileen E 'Children in hospital: do they need a library service?' *Book trolley* 3(3) September, 1971.

THREE

PRISON LIBRARIES:
the historical background

Introduction
THERE ARE certain parallels between the emergence and
the subsequent development of hospital libraries and prison
libraries. These can be summarised:
i) The early collections of books in prisons were frequently
donated by religious bodies. The hope was that the tracts
and sermons, which formed the bulk of this literature, would
lead the prisoners to an awareness of the enormity of their
crimes.
ii) Voluntary bodies were actively concerned with the distribution of reading material to prisons.
iii) A high proportion of the secular works available to the
inmates of prisons consisted of donated books.
iv) The library profession evinced little awareness of the
need to develop viable library services.

Some fundamental differences do exist, however, between
the later progress made by the hospital library movement and
similar events in the evolution of libraries in correctional
institutions. The reasons for this stem from the attitude
which society has towards those who transgress its laws.
The humanitarian spirit which motivated the pioneers in the
hospital library service did not manifest itself when the
desirability of introducing similar facilities into prisons was
discussed.

The doctrine that those in prison have been incarcerated
both as a punishment and as part of their debt to society
has weighed heavily upon attempts to introduce proper

libraries in correctional institutions, and the philosophy, shared by librarians as part of society, that imprisonment should be attended by the maximum discomfort has always precluded the provision of an adequate library service.

The apathy which librarians long displayed towards prison libraries has been compounded by the active hostility which some prison wardens have displayed towards the provision of reading material in their institutions. Books were seen as potential threats to prison discipline and security, introducing dangerous and possibly inflammatory ideas. To bring books into the prisons could lead to unrest and disorder.

In prisons where the establishment of libraries was reluctantly agreed to, severe censorship of reading material has often taken place, and books have been excluded from the institution for the most arbitrary of reasons. It is interesting to compare the attitude of some members of the medical profession to the early development of hospital libraries with the similar distrust shown by prison wardens. The reasons for the antagonism are different, but the effects have been remarkably similar in that the growth of effective library services in both types of institution has long been delayed. And prison officials have found another matter for concern: librarianship is a predominantly feminine profession. The idea of women coming into overwhelmingly male institutions was considered by some prison wardens as a potentially unsettling influence.

The participation of the profession of librarianship in the development of prison library services is not noticeably distinguished. The gradual introduction of libraries in correctional institutions has been the result of the changes which have been taking place in penal philosophy. As more enlightened policies towards the inmates of prisons have evolved, so librarians have progressively extended the services of their libraries. There are few examples of the library profession leading public opinion on the need for proper library provision in prisons. Indeed, many of the early libraries which were established in prisons were brought into being by the efforts of individuals outside the library profession.

A survey of the literature of prison librarianship, conducted by David M Gillespie, shows how little interest there has been in the subject.[1] In all he was only able to trace some five hundred citations on prison library work. He attributes the poor quality of library provision in US correctional institutions to the apathy and indifference of librarians.

There have been changes in recent years, as the library profession has become more aware of the needs of prisoners. This awareness is part of the growing acceptance by librarians that they have a duty to provide a library service to every member of society, whatever their circumstances. The prison authorities, too, are now more favourably disposed towards the provision of reading material to the inmates of correctional institutions. Books are now being accepted as an essential element in the work of rehabilitation.

It would be possible to overstate the improvement which has been made in the quality of prison libraries. There are, as yet, few excellent prison library services in the world, and there are only very small numbers of qualified librarians engaged in prison librarianship. Both the library profession and the prison authorities accept the necessity for properly organised libraries in correctional institutions, but there is, unfortunately, a reluctance to make available the financial resources which would achieve this level of library provision. The history of prison librarianship is punctuated by impassioned assertions of the pressing need for a wide range of books to be available in all prisons. These statements have rarely been accompanied by direct action.

Prison libraries in the United Kingdom
Little attempt was made before the nineteenth century to provide the inmates of prisons with a supply of books. Paradoxically, a number of those imprisoned for religious or political beliefs have used their time in prison to produce outstanding works of literature: Sir Walter Raleigh, John

Bunyan and others have found writing to be a form of solace during their imprisonment. Needless to say, the majority of those finding themselves in prison have lacked the talent or opportunity to indulge in creative writing. Until recently, the major concerns of inmates of penal institutions have been the inadequacies of diet and the primitive sanitary conditions. Absence of writing facilities or reading material would be minor considerations.

In 1877, control and responsibility for prisons passed from local to central government, and this brought some improvements in the lot of prison inmates. One innovation was the introduction of basic education programmes, with arithmetic and writing being taught up to 'standard three'. The prisoners had lessons for two periods of fifteen minutes each a week, with illiterates receiving seventy minutes of instruction. As an incentive, prisoners would be allowed to borrow a book once the required standard of reading was reached.

The Local Prison Code of 1878 had made it a condition that prison libraries would only contain those books which had been approved by the prison commissioner. This was a measure designed to ensure that prisoners would not be exposed to seditious or inflammatory reading material. The prevailing opinion during this period was that access to books was a privilege which had to be earned. This view was reinforced by the 'progressive stage system' devised by Sir Edward Du Cane. This involved a plan whereby the prisoner would proceed in stages, by dint of good conduct, to more congenial work and pleasanter living conditions. Sir Edward's system was also linked to a gradual extension of opportunities for communicating with fellow prisoners, and other privileges accorded to the well-behaved inmate included access to reading material. Here again, the prisoner would progress from one category to another. At first he would be allowed to read the Bible, the second stage would permit him to borrow an educational book, the final stage was the privilege of reading novels and other recreational reading. Frequently short-stay prisoners would leave prison before

59

this final stage was reached, but doubtless their release was some compensation for this disappointment.

By the early twentieth century, a more compassionate policy was being adopted in British correctional institutions. In 1910 Winston Churchill, then the Home Secretary, formed the Departmental Committee on the Supply of Books to Prisons, which examined the whole question of prison libraries. On the basis of the investigations the committee made a number of recommendations. It proposed that the chaplain of each prison should prepare a list of new books suitable for addition to the library, the list to be submitted to the prison commissioners for approval. A grant of 1s 3d per head of the whole prison population was made available for the purchase of books.

The committee also advocated that the subjects embraced by the library should be wider, with the emphasis on moral instruction (the main guide to selection in the past) no longer being the dominant consideration. However, this did not mean the unlimited purchase of recreational material, for the emphasis now was upon educational material.

Since the end of the nineteenth century some attention had been given to the need to improve the basic educational skills of prison inmates and the innovations suggested by the committee were designed to support this work. However, it was acknowledged that the prison library should not consist solely of educational material, and that novels 'both standard and new' should be purchased.

The recommendations of the committee mirrored the growing conviction, held by many concerned with the management of prisons, that the inmates, given the right treatment, could become law abiding and productive members of society. Unfortunately, in spite of the committee's efforts, the numbers of new books added to prison collections was pitifully small. The majority of prison libraries in the country still consisted primarily of a miscellany of items donated by well-wishers, these being supplemented by occasional consignment of books discarded by a neighbouring public library. In an attempt to enliven these moribund collections, many prisons required that inmates receiving gifts of books and magazines would donate them to the library when they had read them.

The strong theological flavour of the earliest libraries had still not been entirely dispelled. In many penal institutions the chaplain was still acknowledged as the custodian of the library, even though the actual distribution of the books to the prisoners was the responsibility of a particular prison officer. Often, the officer in charge of the library would have a number of orderlies drawn from the prisoners, who would take the books to the cells for the other inmates. Direct access to the prison libraries was rarely permitted, instead the prisoners would, in the more enlightened institutions, choose their books from a printed catalogue. In others, the prisoners would have to rely upon the orderlies for the books they wanted. This was, apparently, a system which gave the library orderly considerable power; in return for securing a wanted book for a prisoner he would be able to extort food or tobacco.

The educational programmes which had been introduced in the nineteenth century were continued and strengthened in the early part of the twentieth. In 1923 an application was made to the Carnegie United Kingdom Trust for financial aid, to buy books and to help the voluntary work being undertaken by voluntary teachers in prisons. The trust made an initial grant of £1,000 this being supplemented by a further sum of £750 spread over three years. Official recognition of the value and benefits of the educational work taking place in H M Prisons came with the allocation of £440 by the Treasury for the purchase of textbooks.

With the growing acceptance by the government and other agencies that libraries had a necessary part to play in the rehabilitation of prison inmates, it is chastening to find that this conviction was not apparently shared by librarians. Not until 1936 did the Library Association give some attention to the supply of reading material in prisons. The LA formed a committee to consider ways in which the prison commissioners could be helped and advised on the formation of libraries in prisons. Little practical advice actually emanated from the committee, which largely contented itself with offering suggestions which were, in the context of the times, either inappropriate or unrealistic. For example, it advocated that there should be a professional librarian appointed by the commissioners to coordinate and direct prison library services throughout the country. It is true that an appointment of this kind would have done much to advance the cause of prison libraries, but at a time when the importance of libraries was only just being recognised by the prison authorities, such a far-sighted proposal had little prospect of being accepted.

The committee had also recommended that the Library Association should form a panel of public librarians who would advise on the purchase of books for prisons. This would be done twice a year, lists being submitted to the commissioners. In order to raise the abysmal standard of prison libraries, the capitation grant for the purchase of books should be raised to three shillings.

The prison commissioners' response to these proposals was guarded. A professional librarian was, predictably, not appointed as an adviser but, instead, the post of librarian prisoner officer was created at each prison. The capitation grant was raised to 1s 9d, and the idea of an advisory panel of public librarians was also accepted.

There were other contributions by the British library profession, principally through the efforts of a few public library services. Sometimes more progressive chief librarians would voluntarily extend assistance to prisons in their area, sometimes library services would respond to requests by prison authorities for help and guidance in developing their libraries. The Governor of the Borstal Institution, Mollesby Bay, approached East Suffolk County Library in 1938 seeking assistance with the library service which he was proposing for the young men in the institution. East Suffolk County

Library began by depositing an initial collection of 250 books at the borstal institution. This proved successful, and in 1942 the authority felt the experiment had sufficient merit to be further developed. A grant for this purpose was obtained from the Home Office.

Perhaps the most comprehensive public library service to a prison was provided by Durham County Library which in 1944 accepted complete responsibility for the library in Durham Prison. This proved to be an example which few public libraries felt they could follow. The legislation which governed public libraries in the United Kingdom was imprecise on this issue. It did not specifically authorise the provision of a library to an institution which was not freely accessible to everyone in the community. Prison libraries clearly were not available to everyone, therefore if prison authorities wished public libraries to supply books and other services to penal institutions, then a charge would have to be levied.

The Prison Department of the Home Office was, in fact, prepared to make payments on a per capita basis to public libraries willing to give a service to a prison. Unfortunately the grant would do little more than pay for the books being supplied by the public library. It did, however, offer some encouragement to public libraries. By 1951, fifteen municipal and thirteen county libraries were supplying books and other facilities to prisons in their area. Another eleven authorities were giving a library service to borstal institutions.[2]

Public libraries in the London area were foremost amongst the authorities which, in the immediate post-war years, introduced fully comprehensive library services for penal institutions within their boundaries. Islington Public Library began its services to Pentonville in 1947. It had supplied books before this date but now it was to assume complete responsibility for administering the prison library. This service included a comprehensive bookstock, visits by qualified members of the library staff and access to the support and administrative service of Islington Public Library.

By 1951, Pentonville Branch Library, as the prison collection was named, had a stock of over five thousand books. As a branch of the Islington Public Library Service, the institution was entitled to receive the same level of service available to the other branch libraries in the borough.[3] In 1951 over two hundred and fifty requests for books were received from the inmates of Pentonville and these received the same attention as enquiries from other parts of the library system.[4] The library was administered by a prison officer librarian, with the assistance of prisoner-assistants. To help with the distribution of books to the inmates and advise on the organisation of the library, a professional member of the Islington staff would visit the prison ' . . . on almost every occasion the library is open.'[5]

By 1954, the library at Pentonville prison was loaning a quarter of a million items each year, including music and play sets. Some of the reading material being lent was part of the prison's educational programmes.

Encouraged by this success, Islington extended its services to Holloway, a prison for women. This was not, initially, conducted at the same level as the library at Pentonville, and the collection consisted at first of two hundred books loaned by the public library, these being changed twice a year. In April 1960, the public library was able to assume full responsibility, and a permanent stock of ten thousand volumes was established in the prison, over one third of the books being non-fiction. As with Pentonville, a programme of regular visits by the library's senior professional staff was introduced, apparently a duty which placed a considerable strain upon them.

Penelope Rowlinson, in her investigation of the Islington Public Library service to prisons, found that the capitation grant paid by the Home Office did little more than cover the costs of supplying reading material.[6] Certainly it did not meet the staff costs or the ancillary services which Islington freely supplied. This emphasises the difference of opinion which exists between local authorities and the Home Office.

The latter's view, supported by the prison authorities, is that public libraries have a duty to serve all those resident in their area, including those in correctional institutions. The capitation grant is designed to help public libraries with the costs of giving a library service to prisons; it is not intended to defray all the expenses which the public library will incur. Public libraries feel that the provisions of the Public Libraries and Museums Act of 1964 entitle them to charge for the provision of a library service in a prison on an agency agreement. Until such time as this fundamental disagreement is solved, the quality of library facilities in British prisons will be substantially below those available to the community.

Rowlinson's survey also covered the contributions made by two other London borough libraries to prisons in their locality. Wandsworth and Hammersmith authorities respectively serve Wandsworth Prison and Wormwood Scrubs. Following the example of Islington, both Wandsworth and Hammersmith agreed to accept the prison as a location for one of their branch libraries.[7] The level of service to be given, it was hoped, would be comparable to that available to the rest of the community. The survey reveals a number of factors common to all the prison libraries.[8] In summary these are:

i) A high proportion of the prison population become members of the library. In the case of Wandsworth and Pentonville, every inmate was enrolled as a library user.

ii) The range of books available to the prisoners compares favourably with that generally found in public libraries.

iii) The loan facilities are generous in all the prisons studied, with readers being allowed to borrow in some cases as many as eight books.

iv) Regular visits by full-time members of the public library staff are appreciated and seem to bring some benefits.

v) Censorship is practiced at the insistence of the prison authorities. Books in certain categories are banned as are some individual titles. A more liberal attitude is taken if the process of censorship is in the hands of the prison governor than would be the case if the prison chaplain vetted the books as they were added to the library.

vi) It is accepted as desirable that the prisoners, as far as possible, should be allowed to visit the library. This privilege is subject to security requirements and the size of the prison library. Both factors do in fact reduce the amount of time that prisoners are allowed in choosing books.

Outside London, the growth of prison libraries has been uneven, with a good deal depending upon the enthusiasm of individual chief librarians of public libraries. A survey conducted by the Library Association found that 141 penal institutions were receiving a library service of some kind from public libraries.[9] There were forty-six authorities with a professional librarian organising the service to local prisons. Even so there was no one qualified librarian engaged full-time in this branch of librarianship.[10]

An investigation undertaken by Anne Turner of four prison libraries in the West Riding of Yorkshire confirmed the importance of reading as an activity for prison inmates.[11] She found that ninety-seven per cent of the prisoners included reading in their range of pastimes; literature being obtained from the library or from some other source.[12] In spite of this, the quality of the library facilities in the prisons investigated was generally poor. Anne Turner found that:

i) The library premises were inadequate, with the exception of Wakefield Prison which had a purpose-built library.

ii) The capitation grant, which at the time of the survey was seventy-five pence for each prisoner served, was insufficient to provide even one book for each inmate. Public libraries engaged in the supply of services to prisons found that they would have to augment the collections in the institutions from their own stock. Inevitably, a substantial proportion of the books available to the prison inmates were out-of-date.

iii) The range of subjects embraced by the prison libraries in the survey was limited. The libraries were incapable of giving more than a recreational service.

iv) There were difficulties of communication between

public libraries and prisons. This made it difficult for the staff of the public library to assess whether the books being sent to the prisons were relevant to the needs of the inmates. An associated problem was that few of the requests made by the prisoners for particular items were forwarded to the public libraries. This was in part due to the lack of liaison between the prison and the library staff. The censorship imposed by the prison authorities was, however, almost certainly a contributory factor.

v) Few of the professional staff of the public library were engaged in administering and developing the prison libraries covered by the survey. This meant that the quality of the library service offered to prisoners was low: standard library practice was rarely employed in the prison libraries and few attempts were made to publicise the service.

A later investigation of prison libraries in Scotland was more encouraging.[13] All the Scottish correctional institutions had a library and, in every case, the local public library would be supplementing these collections by the bulk loan of books. Again, however, no qualified librarian was employed in any of the prisons and the administration of the libraries of the institutions was in the hands of prison officers or the prison library staff.

The surveys show the fitful nature of the evolution of prison library services in the United Kingdom. It does reveal that British public libraries have, in the main, accepted that they have a responsibility for the support of prison libraries, and it also indicates the sometimes grudging realisation by prison authorities that a library in a correctional institution has a vital part to play in the rehabilitation of the inmates.

The past decade has seen the development of a working relationship between the library profession and prison authorities on the best means of establishing viable library facilities in correctional institutions. The has led to several reports being published on the most appropriate means of establishing well-organised and properly administered prison libraries. In 1975, for example, the Prison Department of the Home Office received a report of a working party which had been assisted by a library adviser for the Department of Education and Science. The working party did recognise that public libraries were the natural agencies for the supply of library services to correctional institutions. The report also contained a number of other proposals which, if implemented, should provide the basis for a modern and efficient prison library service in Britain.

There are other indications of the developing awareness of prison officers and librarians of the need for immediate action to improve the library facilities for prison inmates. For example, a conference was arranged by the Prison Department of the Home Office in collaboration with the Department of Library and Information Studies at Liverpool Polytechnic in 1976.[14] The conference attracted representatives from public libraries, the prison education service and the prison department. All the speakers at the conference stressed the need for libraries in correctional institutions. There was a recognition of the problems which prison officers and librarians faced. It was suggested that prison officers should receive training in the basic techniques of librarianship, and that librarians concerned with prison libraries should be instructed in the essentials of criminal psychology. The conference agreed that the prison library had both an educational and a recreational role. There was a strong feeling that closer links should be established between the Prison Education Service and public libraries. There was no recommendation made on the need for qualified librarians to be engaged full-time in prisons. This was, perhaps, a tacit recognition that financial and other considerations precluded such a possibility for the immediate future. Instead the conference contented itself with advocating that there should be a prison library officer in every correctional institution who would take sufficient time to ensure that the library facilities were properly available.

Clearly the prison library service in the United Kingdom has to make considerable progress before prison inmates receive a supply of reading material which compares favourably with that available to the rest of the community. The absence of qualified librarians, inadequate premises, moribund book collections are characteristics of too many prison libraries in Britain. A number of sensible proposals have been made, the prison service and the library profession are clearly aware that an efficient, progressive library should be found in every correctional institution. Unfortunately, little, as yet, is being done to implement the many proposals which have been made by prison officers, social workers, teachers and librarians.

Prison libraries in the USA

There is a depressing resemblance between the course of events in America and in Britain, but on balance the former has seen greater progress.

As in Britain, prisons were initially intended to be places of misery and humiliation, and books had no part to play. When they were eventually provided, selection was made on the basis of demonstrating the extent of the prisoners' moral degeneracy: thus the reading material allowed was principally donated by religious organisations, and the accent was upon works leading to regret and repentance. At Philadelphia in 1790, the Prison Society donated a collection of books to the Walnut Street Jail consisting of volumes of prayers, sermons and religious exhortations.[15] The absence of adequate lighting, coupled with the lack of popular appeal of this material, must have deterred all but the most penitent from seeking salvation through these tracts.

By the nineteenth century, more purposeful attempts were being made to establish prison libraries which contained something more than religious works. In 1802, the earliest prison library worthy of the name was established at Kentucky State Penitentiary[16], and this was followed by similar developments in other correctional institutions. Even so, the close association which the prison chaplains had with the administration of libraries ensured that the inmates were still supplied generously with religious works, and their efforts were supported by others anxious that prison inmates should receive a proper exposure to religious thought. Louis Dwight, whose health prevented him from realising his ambitions as a clergyman, sought an alternative career as a distributor of the publications of the American Bible Society. His duties required him to ensure that those in prison were being made aware of the message of the society, and he freely deposited the literature of the American Bible Society in jails and prisons.[17]

Some prison governors, by this time, were adopting a more enlightened approach. Even in the notorious Sing Sing, under the direction of Governor Seward a more enlightened policy saw the introduction of a wider selection of reading material. But the attitude of the prison governor was paramount: at Sing Sing, with a change of governor, the library was abruptly closed, only to resume operations in the same arbitrary manner two years later.

Prison libraries were subject to changes of fortune. During a period of economic expansion, prisons represented a source of cheap labour, and the inmates were engaged for a variety of tasks. If the economy suffered any prolonged recession the need for prison labour was reduced, and alternative methods of occupying prisoners' time had to be found. At Charlestown, Mass, an excellent library was developed to support the prison education programme introduced to replace manual labour. But with a resurgence in the economy, prisoners were again in demand and the library accommodation was converted to workshops.[18] Such fluctuations made a mockery of rehabilitation programmes, and equally reduced the significance of the prison library.

More and more during the nineteenth century the doctrine which saw prison as a place where transgressors against society could be reformed gave way to the popular principle that emphasised punishment rather than rehabilitation. In such a climate of opinion, a library service was seen only as an irrelevancy.

70

Even less progress was made in the case of county jails, which came under the jurisdiction of local authorities. Without the efforts of Linda Gilbert the majority of jails in the United States would have been without library facilities of any kind. Linda Gilbert had become aware, at the age of ten, of the plight of those in county jails.[19] When she inherited her family's fortune she took the opportunity to introduce a library at Cook County Jail which was situated in her home town.[20] This was to be the first step in a life-long campaign to improve the lot of the unfortunates held in county jails.

In addition to committing her own financial resources, Ms Gilbert launched a series of fund-raising activities in order to secure the necessary funds to develop libraries in the county jails. Her achievements were impressive: a library of two thousand books was established in St Louis Jail, two libraries were provided in jails in New York, and, in 1876, she founded the Gilbert Library and Prisoners' Aid Society.[21]

Miriam E Carey was to become an equally important pioneer in prison library development.[22] Her work had its real beginnings with her appointment to the Minnesota Public Library as 'organiser of libraries in institutions', and she worked ceaselessly for the development of the prison libraries in the correctional institutions in that state and in others. In addition, she was actively concerned with the ALA's efforts to encourage prison authorities to introduce properly administered library collections in correctional institutions. One important aspect of this work was Ms Carey's chairing of the ALA Committee on Hospital and Institution Libraries, which established firm links between the library profession and the officers of penal institutions.

The work of this committee had a profound effect on the development of libraries in correctional institutions in the United States. In 1909 it conducted a survey of penal and charitable institutions.[23] The investigation revealed the appalling inadequacy of the book collections in establishments of this kind. In order to secure some improvement in

71

the condition of institutional libraries, the committee laid down two basic principles. These asserted that those in institutions who wished to read had a right to do so, and that if the nature of the institution prevented free access to books, then special provision would have to be made to bring reading material to the inmates.

Throughout the early years of the twentieth century, the committee campaigned vigorously for the establishment of adequate libraries in prisons. It introduced a series of programmes and innovations:[24]

i) It organised exhibitions of reading material which were considered suitable for inclusion in the libraries of correctional institutions.

ii) Periodical surveys were made of the progress being made towards the establishment of properly directed prison libraries.

iii) A manual was published of prison library administration.

iv) Lists of books suitable for incorporation in prison library collections were published.

Gradually, in response to the work of the committee, and other agencies, some progress was made. In 1913 the Prison Association of New York announced that the public library was to provide collections of books in the prisons and jails of the city.[25] Collections of twenty-five to thirty books were despatched to the county jails. Later a series of visits to penal institutions of the city were made by the staff of the New York Public Library. While some of this material had come from the bookstock of the public library, a high proportion had been donated by the citizens of New York.

One year later the State Library was asked by the prison authorities in New York to examine the libraries of a number of correctional institutions.[26] The survey revealed the abysmal state of many of the libraries in the prisons and jails: the bookstock was usually completely inadequate, and the libraries were, in many cases, under the control of the chaplain or prison superintendent which meant in effect that the collections were largely unsupervised. The library made a

72

number of highly practical recommendations for improving the organisation, but these proposals went almost totally unheeded. This was to be a common fate of recommendations made by agencies intent on improving the standards in the libraries of correctional institutions.

Not unnaturally, perhaps, little progress was made in prison library reform during the First World War, but the end of hostilities did bring a quickening of interest. The ALA conference of 1919 saw the formation of the Committee on Enlarged Programs for American Library Service.[27] As part of its campaign for library reform, the new committee advocated that the ALA should do all it could to promote the establishment of libraries in correctional institutions, irrespective of whether these were administered by federal, state or local government. A sum of $25,000 was set aside by the ALA to finance a campaign to draw the country's attention to the urgent need for proper library facilities in prisons.

In spite of this strong advocacy for reform, very little was actually accomplished. The library profession in the United States paid little heed to the exhortations of its own body. An attempt by the Committee on Institution Libraries to assemble a pilot prison library project had to be abandoned for lack of financial support.

During the inter-war years, individuals did as much good as committees. The work of Austin H MacCormick contributed in no small part to the steady reform of prison libraries. In 1927 he had been appointed Assistant Director to the United States Bureau of Prisons with direct responsibility for education and libraries. In the same year, with the aid of a grant from the Carnegie Foundation, Austin MacCormick accompanied Paul W Garrett, Executive Secretary of the National Society of Penal Information (now the Osborne Association) on a survey of the educational provision being made in US prisons.

The findings of the survey formed the substance of his book *The education of adult prisoners—a survey and a program*.[28] A chapter of this was devoted to an evaluation of the role of the library in a correctional institution, and damningly indicted the existent services. In the opinion of MacCormick, the majority of the books in these collections were only fit to be thrown away. Few institutions had anything approaching an adequate stock of books, in fact in most collections anything up to ninety per cent of the books were obsolete.

There was a shortage of professional librarians working in the field. Usually the prison chaplain would act as librarian in addition to his other duties, but those responsible for the library in a prison could be drawn from a variety of occupations. Teachers, prison officers, even clerical workers could be asked to watch over the collection of books.

In very few prisons were the inmates allowed access to the library. Their selection of reading material would have to be made from a duplicated list of the stock of the library. Invariably the library premises would be cramped, the majority being situated in converted cells. In some of the newer prisons the library might be located near the education and recreation areas but in the majority of institutions the libraries were badly sited and in unsuitable accommodation.

MacCormick's report did include a series of recommendations for improving the quality of prison libraries in the United States. He stressed the value of publicity in stimulating the use of the library. There should be proper financial support and trained librarians should be employed. He advocated, perhaps unrealistically in the context of the times, that those who were recruited to the prison library service should have a knowledge of sociology, criminology, psychiatry and psychology. The report also contained criticisms of the censorship policies which operated in many institutions.

But MacCormick's recommendations met the fate of similar proposals. Little attempt was made to implement the advice, although the section in the work on prison librarianship does now have a firm place in the literature.

There were, however, important changes taking place in the role of the prison library in US correctional institutions.

74

By 1940 prison libraries were becoming more closely identified with the educational provision being made for prisoners. This could mean, in some, that the budgets for the library and the educational programmes were linked, which brought some benefits for the library. It also meant that the control of the library and its selection policies passed to the teaching staff.

This change in emphasis did not bring any immediate improvements in the quality of bookstocks or facilities. A survey published in 1941 revealed that little progress had been made since the MacCormick investigations fourteen years earlier.[29] The main findings of the 1941 survey were:

i) Only fifty per cent of the prisons responding to the enquiry were making specific provision in their budgets for a library. The amount allocated to individual prison libraries would vary considerably: one library was receiving three thousand dollars for the purchase of books for the 1500 inmates, another was spending fifty dollars per annum on its library which served one thousand prisoners.

ii) In general the library services in federal prisons reached a higher standard than those in the state penitentiaries.

iii) There were few trained librarians employed in the prison libraries and only one full-time professional librarian was working in the state prisons. In fifty-five correctional institutions the director of education nominally acted as librarian, while, in twenty-five others, the chaplain included the library in his list of responsibilities. Only in one-third of the institutions covered by the survey were librarians organising library services.

iv) The poor quality of many prison libraries did not deter the inmates from making use of them. In some institutions the entire prison population was enrolled as members of the library; elsewhere it was not uncommon to find over half the inmates being regular users of the library.

v) A high proportion of the books were worn out with anything up to ninety per cent fit only to be discarded.

By this time another body was adding its voice to the campaign to secure effective library provision in prisons. In

75

1941 the American Prison Association (APA) had created its own committee on prison libraries. Three years later the APA Committee on Institutional Libraries published *Objectives and standards for libraries in adult prisons and reformatories*.[30] The basic recommendations were that there should be a full-time civilian librarian employed in every prison with one to two thousand inmates; that there should be a minimum of ten books per inmate and that two thousand dollars should be allocated each year for the purchase of new books.

A number of surveys conducted during the 1950s suggested that the standards recommended by the APA were rarely being reached. Edwin Friedman, in a study published in 1950, was particularly scathing in his observations on the quality of prison libraries.[31] He noted that, while the majority of state and federal prisons had a library, a high proportion of the books they contained consisted of donated material and frequently the prisoners had to organise their own library service. Other surveys, published between 1950 and 1960, confirmed these criticisms.

As late as 1959 Harry Elmer Barnes and Negley K Teeters described prison libraries in terminology reminiscent of Mac-Cormick, Souter and other earlier writers.[32] They condemned US correctional institution libraries as repositories of worn-out and unsuitable reading material, lacking both resources and trained staff.

It would be giving too depressing a picture to suggest that no progress was made during the years between the two world wars. In some states, attempts had been made to improve the quality of library provision. This was particularly apparent where the prison authorities had embarked upon extensive rehabilitation programmes. In 1944 California embarked upon an ambitious programme of penal reform which brought substantial improvements in the quality of the libraries in the state prisons. The library was seen both as a source of educational and vocational information and as a means of developing the prisoners' cultural and artistic interests. The quality of prison library provision in the immediate postwar years was considerably ahead of that being achieved in other states. Gradually the example provided by California and the stimulus given by the ALA and other associations began to have an impact upon the standards of prison library services.

The ALA had demonstrated its growing concern by amalgamating the Institution Libraries Committee with the Division of Hospital Libraries to form the Association of Hospital and Institution Libraries (AHIL), now the Health and Rehabilitative Services Division. This change was designed to give the subject of prison librarianship a greater significance in the activities of the association. It also gave an outlet for articles and discussions on prison library work through the Division's own journal the *AHIL quarterly* (now the *HRLSD journal*).

These changes in the structure of the ALA were effected in 1956, and this date saw a growth of interest at state level in the provision of reading material to correctional institutions. By 1959 four state libraries had begun to supply books to prisons through their mobile library services, while eight state library associations had formed committees to examine the possibilities for developing libraries in correctional institutions.

The 1960s saw a quickening of activity following the establishment of the Association of Hospital and Institution Libraries. In 1965, AHIL with the American Correctional Association produced the *Inventory of libraries in state and federal correctional institutions*.[33] It was a timely investigation, coinciding with the preliminary discussions which were taking place before the passing of the Library Services and Construction Act. Senator Javits was able to make use of the statistical evidence in the AHIL/ACA survey to press home his support for federal aid for institution libraries.

Opinion in the United States is divided on the impact which the act had upon the development of libraries in correctional institutions. An amended version, as approved in 1966, made provision for participating states to receive an initial sum of seven thousand dollars each for the fiscal year 1966/67 to improve prison libraries. In the following year this was to be forty thousand dollars for the same purpose.

There is little doubt that the act did bring some improvements to libraries in correctional institutions. But the low level of service provided by many prison libraries required the expenditure of much greater sums than those being made available through it.

A survey conducted by the California Institute of Library Research with the aid of a grant of $77,000 from the US Office of Education[34] reviewed the progress made in previous years, and concluded that there were only three library programmes in correctional institutions which could be regarded as successful. For the most part the story of prison library development was a saga of committees appointed and making recommendations which were fated to go largely unheeded.

In 1972 Dr Lesta Burt published the results of a similar survey which she had made of correctional institution libraries.[35] Her findings were broadly similar to those of the California Institute: the Library Services and Construction Act had succeeded in improving the overall quality of library provision, but the majority of prison libraries were inadequately funded, and badly organised. Few institutions attempted to stimulate the use of the libraries by programmes of library related activities.

Even in California, which has made a distinguished contribution to the furtherance of prison libraries, it was revealed that the standard of book collections was variable. In 1973 the Blue Ribbon Committee on Correctional Library Services submitted a series of recommendations to the Director of the California Department of Corrections.[36] In doing so it provided a critique of existing provision. The committee found that the majority of prisons lacked an adequate prison service. It referred to the heavy reliance upon donated material, and the absence of planned programmes for selecting new material for the libraries. The emphasis was upon quantity rather

78

than quality in building up library collections, and this was compounded by a general lack of concern for the physical condition of the reading material. The committee advocated (echoing many other reports and surveys) that many prison libraries would be well-advised to discard much of their book-stock. Few libraries made adequate provision for non-book materials; gramophone records, tapes and films were rarely supplied. The committee did acknowledge that several of the libraries in the California correctional institutions were trying to meet the reading needs of ethnic minority groups.

The committee examined the vexed question of inmates' access to legal material. It considered the implications of the Gilmore v Lynch court case (see page 94), which carried the clear implication that prison inmates had the right to consult legal material relevant to their case and their appeals. The committee felt that the supply of legal books was subject to practical difficulties. After consulting a number of interested groups, including the prisoners, the committee concluded that a centralised collection of legal works would be the best solution. This would avoid unnecessary duplication, it would also ensure that the collection was administered by librarians skilled in the handling of legal material.

One of the most valuable parts of the Blue Ribbon Report is the definition which it gives of the purpose of a library in a correctional institution:

i) It should act as a support agency for the educational work of the institution.

ii) It should meet the recreational needs of the inmates, assist the prisoners in their private study and supply their general reading interests.

iii) The library should support those programmes which are designed to secure the rehabilitation of the inmates.

iv) The library should provide a reference centre where prisoners can bring their legal problems.

It is apparent from the many investigations and reports which have been made in recent times, that the contribution which a library can make to a correctional institution is widely acknowledged. The fundamental difficulty has been in securing the necessary financial support to implement the recommendations made by the many committees which have deliberated on prison library provision.

As in the United Kingdom, the library profession and prison officers have been working together to improve standards. In 1966 the ALA and the ACA established a joint working party to examine prison libraries and there have been a number of cooperative ventures between the two associations. In 1972, for example, they jointly published (through the ALA's Health and Rehabilitative Library Services Division) *Library standards for juvenile correctional institutions*.[37]

Conclusion

There have been some advances made, particularly in the last two decades, in the formation of properly administered libraries in American correctional institutions. There are more professional librarians engaged in this branch of librarianship; there is a greater awareness of the library as an adjunct to the educational, vocational and rehabilitation programmes being provided in the modern institution. The series of recommendations contained in the reports, surveys and published standards, has had some effect on the quality of libraries in US prisons. In spite of this the level of service in the majority of prison libraries in the United States, as in many other parts of the world, rarely approaches that available in the community. Indeed the average prison library is often markedly inferior to those which have been established in hospitals.

The following chapter advances a rationale for properly administered, adequately financed prison libraries. It will indicate the role which a fully-equipped library service can play in a correctional institution.

REFERENCES
1 Gillespie, David M 'A citation-entry analysis of the literature on prison libraries' *AHIL quarterly* 8 spring 1968, 65-72.

2 Watson, Richard Fell *Prison libraries* London, LA, 1951 (LA pamphlet no 7), 17.

3 Islington Public Library *Annual report 1951-52*, 13.

4 Ibid, 13.

5 Ibid, 14.

6 Rowlinson, Penelope A 'Survey of the provision and use of library services in certain London prisons' in *Provision and use of library and documentation services: some contributions from the University of Sheffield*. Postgraduate School of Librarianship, edited by W L Saunders. Pergamon Press, 1966, 79.

7 Ibid, 67, 70.

8 Ibid, 72-82.

9 Library Association *Library and information bulletin* 1(4), 1967, 118.

10 Ibid, 117.

11 Turner, Anne 'Library services in four West Riding prisons' *Howard journal of penology and crime prevention* 13(4), 1973, 288-296.

12 Ibid, 293.

13 Hunter, Margaret W T 'Libraries in Scottish prisons' *Book trolley* 2(3), September 1968, 58-60.

14 Savage, Janice 'One day conference on prison libraries 17th March 1976 at Liverpool' Cumbria County Library *Viewpoint* 8, April 1976, 4-6.

15 Engelbarts, Rudolf *Books in stir* Metuchen (NJ), Scarecrow Press, 1972, 26.

16 Rubin, Rhea Joyce *US prison library services and their theoretical base* University of Illinois, Graduate School of Library Sciences, 1973, Occasional paper no 110.

17 Reynolds, Ruth Caroline *The role of librarianship in penal institutions: an historical review and survey of contemporary training programs* Thesis presented to the Faculty of the Department of Librarianship, California State University, San José, 1973, 20.

18 Ibid, 20-21.

19 Ibid, 22.

20 Ibid, 22.

21 Ibid, 23.

22 MacCormick, Austin H *A brief history of libraries in American correctional institutions* Proceedings of the American Correctional Association, Cincinnati, October 12, 1970, 200.

23 Report of the Committee on Commission work in State Institutions. American Library Association Bulletin, September, 1909. (Cited in Reynolds op cit, 2).

24 Reynolds op cit, 28.

25 'Prison libraries' *Library journal* November 1915, 841.

26 Reynolds op cit, 37.

27 Preliminary Report of the American Committee on Enlarged Programs for American Library Services. *American Library Association bulletin*, September 1919, 653-654.

28 MacCormick, Austin H *The education of adult prisoners* New York, National Society of Penal Information, 1931.

29 Souter, S H 'Results of a prison library survey' in: American Prison Association *Proceedings of the 71st annual conference, San Francisco August 19th-22nd, 1941.* New York, American Prison Association, 322-327.

30 American Prison Association, Committee on Institutional Libraries 'Objectives and standards for libraries in adult prison and reformatories'. (Cited in MacCormick *Brief history*, op cit, 204.

31 Friedman, Edwin 'Survey shows poor libraries in most penal institutions' *Library journal* 75, July 1950, 1148-1149.

32 Barnes, Harry Elmer and Negley, K Teeter *New horizons in criminology* 3rd ed Englewood Cliffs, Prentice-Hall, 1959, 346.

33 American Correctional Association and Association of Hospital and Institution Libraries *Inventory of library resources in correctional institutions* August 1965.

34 Rubin op cit, 9.

35 Burt, Lesta Norris 'Keepers of men need keepers of books' *Crime and delinquency* 18(3) July 1972, 271-283.

36 California Library Association Blue Ribbon Committee on Correctional Library Services *Report to the director of the California Department of Corrections* July 1973, Sacramento, California Library Association, 1973.

37 American Correctional Association/American Library Association (HRLSD) Joint Committee on Institutional Libraries *Library standards for juvenile correctional institutions* ACA/ALA, 1975.

FOUR

PRISON LIBRARIES:
organisation and administration

Penal systems

THE ESTABLISHMENT of library services in correctional institutions needs to be related to the differing penal systems which operate in various parts of the world. In the United Kingdom, correctional institutions for adults are controlled by the central government through the Home Office, responsibility being exercised by the Prison Department. In the United States there is a more complex penal system with correctional institutions administered by either the federal, state or local government.

The term 'correctional' or 'penal' can be used to describe different categories of institution. In most countries there are several types of correctional institution which will differ both in their function and in the category of offender provided for. However, certain aspects are shared by all such establishments. Inmates are compelled to lead lives which are severely circumscribed by the twin requirements of security and discipline. This insistence upon security and closely regulated behaviour imposes an atmosphere which is unsympathetic to the establishment of library services. The concept of a library implies that there will be free access to books, and this is allied to the ideal that the individual has a right to read any material which is available in printed form. In the past, prisons have rarely provided these unconditional liberties. It is the reforms which have taken place in penal institutions in this country which have introduced an environment in which libraries have a definite place. The more draconian features of prison life have been eliminated and there have been a number of important innovations.

There is greater emphasis in modern prisons upon the rehabilitation of inmates. Educational and vocational programmes have been introduced to help the prisoners when they leave. The planning and design of prisons built in recent years has been more imaginative: the more institutional features of the early prisons are no longer acceptable in the modern penal establishment. Today professional workers are attached to prisons; these include teachers, social workers and psychiatrists. The acceptance that those from these and other occupations can assist in the rehabilitation of the prison inmate has provided the right background to consider the need for qualified librarians in prisons.

In spite of this far-reaching reappraisal of the basic purposes of correctional institutions, there are aspects of life in penal establishments which make it difficult to provide effective library services.

There are to begin with the simple difficulties caused by the living conditions of many prisons, for a high proportion of correctional institutions are overcrowded. There has, for example, been a twenty-two per cent increase in the number of young prisoners committed to prisons in the United Kingdom. In 1976 the prison population accommodated two or three to a cell. This is hardly conducive to reading more than the simplest of books. It also means that the area allocated to the library will often be severely restricted, making it difficult to provide more than a recreational service.

Another aspect of the prison community which distinguishes it from the rest of society is that the population is of one sex. Other factors which distinguish the prison community include the predominance, in all-male institutions, of young offenders. As Michael Wolff says, it is the youthfulness of the inmates which initially surprises visitors to prisons.[1] Margaret Shaw, in her investigation of Gartree and Ashwell correctional institutions, found that half the men at

Gartree and one-third of the men at Ashwell were under thirty.[2] Marjorie Le Donne has noted the same characteristic in correctional institutions in the United States with over ninety-five per cent of the state and federal prison population being men and juvenile offenders comprising over one-third of the male inmates.[3]

Le Donne also refers to the high proportion of the prison population in the United States who are members of ethnic minority groups. Black Americans and those from the Spanish-speaking sections of American society are to be found in US correctional institutions in disproportionate numbers.[4] This is also true of American Indians who comprise a much higher percentage of those in prison than the size of the Indian community would seem to warrant.[5] There are disquieting indications that the same trends are emerging in the United Kingdom with members of minority groups, particularly the West Indians being committed to correctional institutions in increasing numbers. The social factors which are contributing to this are not dissimilar from those which exist in the United States.

Another characteristic which differentiates the prison community from the rest of society is that many of those sentenced are mentally disturbed. Gibbens found in his study of borstals that twenty-seven per cent of the inmates were mentally abnormal.[6]

The standards of education reached by those in prison are frequently lower than those attained by the rest of the community. Le Donne cites the position in US correctional institutions where, in 1960, over half the adult inmates had not received a high school education.[7] Banks presents a similar picture in British prisons and borstals, where the inmates often had failed to attain a reasonable standard of education.[8] However, Gibbens draws attention to the results of intelligence tests conducted with borstal inmates. These indicate that the level of intelligence of those in correctional institutions does not differ significantly from the rest of the population.[9] This would suggest that many of the inmates of correctional institutions have the intelligence to benefit from general education programmes.

Libraries in prisons

Although there are difficulties in organising a supply of reading material, the prison library will, almost invariably, attract considerable use. Rubin records that twice the proportion of inmates in American prisons read books as compared to the rest of the population.[10] It is evident, too, that reading as an activity does bring considerable benefits to those who are imprisoned. Suvak claims that reading can be a catalyst for emotional release for prison inmates as well as satisfying more mundane purposes of providing information or acting as a source of entertainment.[11] The value of literature in establishing, or re-establishing, the inmates' identity is indicated by Gulker, who also notes the value of books as a means of escaping from the stress of life in a correctional institution.[12]

The educational role:

It was suggested earlier that the development of educational programmes in correctional institutions has influenced the growth of supporting library services. This trend seems more apparent in the United States than in Britain. Rubin emphasises the rehabilitative role of the library which has, he considers, superseded all other functions in significance.[13] Le Donne suggests that libraries in many American correctional institutions are seen merely as adjuncts to the educational programmes. She draws attention to the situation in those institutions administered by the Federal Bureau of Prisons.[14] Here the library is regarded as a multi-media agency whose main function is to support the work of educating the detainees. Their recreational needs are met by deposit collections of paperbacks situated near the living quarters. This relegates the recreational and cultural role of the library to a minor position, and in doing so ignores the value of such provision in helping the self-development of

86

the inmates. It does not take account of the contribution which the library can make to overcoming long periods of boredom, an unavoidable feature of prison life.

This has not, as yet, become an obvious issue in the United Kingdom. It is perhaps true that some of the teaching staff in British correctional institutions would like to see the library more directly under their control. Stratta regrets that libraries in borstals have become more associated with leisure than with educational programmes.[15] British librarians would certainly subscribe to the view that the library has a duty to support the educational and vocational teaching activities of a correctional institution. They would, however, see the educational role of the library as just one facet of its work and not an overriding purpose. Few would accept that a library in any institution should be administered by members of another profession. This may be compelled by circumstances; it should not be regarded as an ideal.

Remedial education:
There will be prisoners whose standard of general education is low, and some may be functionally illiterate. Between ten and twenty-five per cent of the inmates of the average British prison have a reading age of eleven or lower. In British correctional institutions there are up to ten thousand inmates who need remedial education in basic reading, writing and numeracy skills. This has necessitated that an important part of the educational work in British prisons be directed towards remedial education.

There is an apparent statistical correlation between the commission of criminal offences and low educational standards. This underlines the importance of remedial education in correctional institutions, both for the inmate and for society. The library in a prison can assist inmates receiving remedial reading instruction by supplying a range of easy to read books. The prisoner may wish to read the books in the library as they may be subject to ridicule by their cell mates if they are seen reading books with simple wording. It has to

87

be accepted that in prisons with strict security regulations this may not be feasible. Nevertheless literature of this kind should be available and it should be possible to supplement the collection from public or other libraries.

The library can also assist the tutor conducting the remedial reading classes by supplying educational aids including flash cards and games involving word skills. This is perhaps the ideal arrangement. In practice, given the absence of qualified or even trained librarians in British prisons, the control of educational material of this kind will usually be invested in the teaching staff of the institution rather than the library.

Vocational education:

Great importance is attached to vocational training in many prisons, borstals and some detention centres. Trade training is seen as a means whereby the inmate, on returning to society, will have acquired skills which will be of use when seeking employment. The evidence which is available does not wholly support this optimism. Former prison inmates do experience difficulty in finding work enabling them to utilise the knowledge which they have gained from vocational courses undertaken during their period of imprisonment. However, the movement away from traditional prison occupations, such as sewing mail-bags and similar tedious pursuits, does go some way towards making existence in prison more interesting and more purposeful.

The creation of vocational courses of this kind will stimulate a demand for reading material to supplement the practical instruction received at the work bench. The range of books which will be needed to support the vocational programmes will often be beyond the resources of the institution's library, particularly those restricted by lack of space and adequate financial support. Many British correctional institutions rely upon the cooperation of public libraries in meeting requests for particular books on technical or commercial subjects. The public library may be receiving a per capita grant from the Prison Department for supplying services on an agency basis. In these cases the public library may consider depositing a collection of technical literature in the prison library. This collection can be used to meet the immediate needs of those inmates pursuing vocational courses. More advanced textbooks can be supplied through the public library request service to the prison.

Some detainees may be pursuing individual courses of study in educational or vocational fields. This may require access to prescribed readings which will normally not be found in the library of the institution. The solution again will be to draw upon the resources of another library which is willing to meet requests for specific titles.

Recreational reading:

The type of correctional institution and the categories of inmate which it contains will influence the type of library service to be provided. In local prisons and remand centres, where the inmate population will be largely transient, the emphasis will be upon recreational reading. The predominant role of the library will be to supply those books which give some relief from the boredom the prisoners will suffer when they are confined to their cells for long periods. Light fiction and books which are both entertaining and exciting will be welcomed. The conditions in which the inmates are living, and the probability that few will have sophisticated reading tastes, will preclude the provision of books of a more demanding nature. Those who are awaiting sentencing will usually lack the will and concentration to read books which require the exercise of real attention.

Paperback books are suitable for library collections in institutions where a high proportion of the inmates are remanded for sentencing or transfer to other establishments. The hard-back book will, in some instances, arouse some resistance if it is associated in the minds of the inmates with academic pursuits. The paperback takes up little space, a matter of some importance in prison libraries with limited

89

accommodation. Paperbacks, too, are relatively inexpensive, a factor in institutions with a shifting population which can cause a high loss rate.

Recreational reading, especially of fiction works, will also occupy a significant place in the bookstock of the correctional institution library serving long-term inmates. Gulker's survey of the fiction titles most suitable for inclusion in a prison library does suggest that the reading tastes of the inmates of correctional institutions can be as diverse as those found in the community as a whole.[16]

Inevitably, as Gulker's findings were based upon experience gained in US prisons, those books found to be the most popular were usually by American authors. Baldwin, Miller, Wright, Ellison and Parks were amongst the writers in the greatest demand in American prison libraries. Similarly the range of interests expressed by the inmates' requests for books reflect the multi-racial character of US society. 'Black literature' and other books dealing with the culture of ethnic minority groups were in heavy demand.

In the UK, Kathryn Lutas has provided a description of the reading tastes of the inmates of Strangeways prison.[17] A good supply of fiction was found to be crucially important, particularly westerns and mystery stories as this represented the only type of literature which some of the inmates would read. The social background of the inmates apparently determined their reading tastes. Books on soccer and boxing were popular, those covering the middle-class sports of golf and cricket were largely ignored. The accepted masters of English fiction had a small but faithful following, while books of poetry were frequently consulted in search of suitable quotations to be included in letters to wives or sweethearts.

Investigations conducted into the reading interests of the inmates of correctional institutions reveal some distinctive preferences. Gulker found a considerable demand for autobiographical and biographical works which embraced the lives of contemporary folk-heroes such as Malcolm X, Sammy

Davis Jnr, and John F Kennedy. Historical figures, such as Washington and Jefferson, however, received only marginal attention.[18] Gulker's survey does show how much national and ethnic factors affect the attention which particular public figures command. Although Kathryn Lutas does note the popularity of biographical material,[19] it is reasonable to suppose that the folk-heroes at Strangeways differ from those of American prisons.

Gulker found that material dealing with historical themes, poetry and drama, philosophy and religion were not in great demand. Reference books, and text-books aiding writing and spelling were widely used which, Gulker suggests, indicates that the library in a correctional institution can help the inmates in their everyday life.[20]

Censorship

One obvious manifestation of the preoccupation with security is the restraint which is placed upon certain categories of reading material. There has been some relaxation of the former rigid surveillance to which the prison authorities used to subject books added to libraries, but nevertheless, even in the most liberal of institutions, the library will be subject to some form of censorship. Rubin has identified some of the categories of reading material which prison authorities have considered to be unsuitable.[21] Westerns have been excluded from some because it was felt that they would encourage inmates to adopt anti-social attitudes and perhaps lead to a contempt for law and order. Detective stories were also distrusted because they would often provide graphic descriptions of criminal techniques which, presumably, could be put into practice once the prisoner was released. Newspapers have been banned as they contain accounts of felonies. Political works have, at different times, been excluded from prison library collections. Medical literature is often not permitted in case the prisoners learn the symptoms of illnesses in order to malinger. Books with graphic sexual passages are rarely allowed.

Prison authorities are inclined to overreact to printed material which they feel could endanger prison security. The anxiety which unfamiliar literature in a prison library can cause is emphasised by the alarm which the inclusion of Spanish language books caused in some US correctional institutions. As the prison staff lacked the necessary linguistic knowledge to read works in Spanish, the books could not be effectively censored.

British prisons have similar policies for excluding certain categories of literature. The Prison Department of the Home Office has listed a number of subjects which it feels should not be represented in British prison libraries. Individual governors of prisons can, and often do, impose their own restraints upon books which they consider to be potentially harmful to order and discipline in the institutions under their control.

Kathryn Lutas has categorised the books which are excluded automatically from the stock of the prison library at Strangeways:[22]

i) Books containing maps of the United Kingdom, particularly those of the area around the prison. It being considered that maps and plans of this kind could be useful to those contemplating escape.

ii) Medical books are prohibited for the same reasons advanced by the US prison authorities: the inmates might use the information to be obtained from books of this type to simulate illness in order to avoid some unpleasant duty.

iii) Books dealing with radio technology are withheld as they might be used to obtain the necessary information to transform receivers into 'walkie-talkie' devices. These could be used to make contact with accomplices outside the institution when planning an escape.

There are other types of book which have not, as a matter of policy, been added to the stock of prison libraries. These include books on karate, works which encourage 'introspection', material on psychology. Literature can be censored by prison authorities for the most arbitrary reasons and it is clear that inmates of correctional institutions are denied access to books which are freely available to the rest of the community.

This could be interpreted as a deliberate attempt to emphasise to the prisoners that they have forfeited certain of their civic rights. In truth, the reasons for not allowing certain works into a prison library are, almost invariably, associated with the need to preserve security and internal discipline.

Librarians have rarely questioned the right of prison authorities to impose sanctions upon the books which the prisoners wish to read. A contributory factor is the lack of interest which the library professional generally has shown in prison librarianship, and a further problem is that the responsibility for the selection of books for a library in a correctional institution will frequently be in the hands of a prison officer—who will naturally subscribe to the penal philosophy which governs the establishment.

The few successful challenges which have been made to the practice of censorship in prisons have been made by the inmates themselves. In the United States in recent years legal decisions have made it possible for Black Muslims to read 'Muhammad speaks' and other Black Muslim works while they are in prison. Black Panthers awaiting trial were able to secure the right to read their own newspapers as a direct result of a court hearing.

Prisons are unique institutions, in which there is a necessary concern with security, but some of the decisions banning certain categories of literature have verged upon the capricious and owe little to reason and commonsense. Now that a more enlightened attitude is being taken towards the prison library, librarians could do much to change the attitudes of prison authorities. This could be accomplished through frank discussions about censorship between librarians and prison governors. At the present time it seems that the library profession is disposed to accept unquestioningly the assumption by the authorities that the inmates of correctional institutions

93

should be denied rights which other members of society enjoy.

Legal collections

The desirability of prisoners having free access to law literature is an issue which has arisen primarily in the United States. This is the result of a series of decisions taken by the federal and state courts, with the famous Gilmore v Lynch case in 1971 acting as the initial catalyst. This was an action taken by the inmates of correctional institutions in California against rules which denied them access to legal materials. The case was fought in the California State Legislature with the court finding for the prisoners. The decision was upheld in the Supreme Court in Younger v Gilmore (E Younger having replaced T Lynch as Attorney General). The implication of Younger v Gilmore was that the US Supreme Court had established the constitutional right of those in prison to gain access to legal materials.

In practice, the inmates of prisons have not been able to obtain all the law books which they need. While all federal correctional institutions have some legal material available, the state prisons' law collections are often inadequate. At least six per cent of state prisons, according to a survey conducted by O James Werner, had no law material available. Werner[23] felt that this figure could in fact be higher. Few of the legal collections in correctional institutions are supervised by trained personnel, and over two-thirds of the institutions refused the inmates the right to take law books from the library. Many such law collections lacked even the basic reference books.

Before the prison library accepts responsibility for the provision of legal information it is necessary to determine whether such a facility is absolutely necessary. The cost of maintaining a collection of law books will be considerable. Such books are expensive, and if the collection is to be effective, it will need to constantly be revised to reflect the changes which take place in statute law. The prisoners will

94

need assistance from a person skilled in handling law literature and, preferably, some knowledge of the law. This presupposes that the prison librarian will have a detailed proficiency in dealing with legal enquiries. An alternative is to have a qualified lawyer available at certain times to help with complex cases. Few correctional institutions have libraries where this level of assistance is available.

There are other difficulties: there is the general hostility of prison authorities, who consider that unrestricted access to legal material in correctional institutions could constitute a threat to security. In spite of this a strong case can be made for the maintenance of a collection of basic legal material in correctional institutions. Celeste MacLeod has suggested some occasions when prison inmates could find law books invaluable[24] —in considering a post-conviction appeal, for instance. Law books can help prison inmates with the civil problems which imprisonment has caused: divorce actions, child custody and social security problems. The prisoner may feel that their rights are not being properly observed, having been placed in solitary confinement without proper cause, or they may not be receiving proper medical attention.

The answer may lie in a compromise, where prisoners do have a right to consult legal material, but such collections would be held in a central location rather than in every prison.

The prison librarian

There are relatively few professional librarians working in a full-time capacity in the field of prison librarianship. A number of factors have contributed to this situation. It is, in part, a natural result of the lack of interest which the library profession has shown towards the provision of libraries in correctional institutions. Prison authorities have been equally slow to acknowledge the value of properly administered library services. The poor salaries and career opportunities in prison library work, coupled with the difficult and often circumscribed conditions have deterred all but the most dedicated.

The absence of professional librarians has meant that the growth of prison libraries has been fragmentary and ill-directed. The US Federal Bureau of Prisons and some state departments of correction have, in recent years, attempted to correct this by appointing librarians to act as coordinators of prison library development. There have been some encouraging results from this where library coordinators have been able to solve some administrative problems. They have been active in encouraging the use of established library techniques and, in the process, develop prison library services which are founded upon sound library principles.[25]

In the United Kingdom the Library Association had proposed as early as 1936 that there should be a librarian to the Home Office to coordinate prison library development in Britain. This suggestion was not accepted and the subsequent history of prison library evolution is one of neglect and apathy. Progress in the years since the end of the Second World War has hinged upon the willingness of public libraries to act as agencies for the supply of books and other material assistance to prisons. This has brought professional librarians into the field of prison library work, but not as prison librarians. Apart from the isolated examples of institutions for the criminally insane, there are no professional librarians working full-time in British correctional institutions.

The practice of prison librarianship is almost totally unexplored. There are few educational and training programmes for those wishing to specialise in this aspect of library work. Ruth C Reynolds has given an account of some of the educational programmes which have been offered in American schools of librarianship.[26] These show imagination and some have the additional merit of bringing the students into direct contact with conditions in correctional institutions.

British library schools have not introduced any significant programmes in prison librarianship. The training opportunities for those engaged in this branch of library work are few. The reluctance of library schools to give more than passing attention to the subject is undoubtedly related to the scant attention which prison libraries have received from the profession as a whole. This is a mistaken policy; there is an urgent need for young librarians to be informed of the pressing necessity for properly endowed, correctly administered library services in correctional institutions.

REFERENCES

1 Wolff, Michael *Prison: the penal institutions of Britain—prisons, borstals, detention centres, attendance centres, approved schools and remand homes* London, Eyre and Spottiswoode, 1967, 29.

2 Shaw, Margaret *Social work in prisons: an experiment in the use of extended contact with offenders* Home Office Research Studies, London, HMSO, 1974, 36.

3 Le Donne, Marjorie 'The role of the library in a correctional institution' *Library and information services for special groups* (ed) Joshua I Smith. Science Associates/International Inc, 1974, 265.

4 Ibid, 265-266.

5 Ibid, 266.

6 Gibbens, T C N *Psychiatric studies of borstal lads* London, OUP, 1963, 201.

7 Le Donne op cit, 266.

8 Banks, Frances *Teach them to live* London, Max Parrish, 1958, 67-68.

9 Gibbens op cit, 202.

10 Rubin op cit, 2.

11 Suvak, Daniel S *Prison inmate attitudes towards reading and library facilities* Masters research paper submitted to Kent University, School of Library Science, 1972, 2-10.

12 Culkor, Virgil *Books behind bars* Metuchen (NJ), Scarecrow Press, 1973, 13-14.

13 Rubin op cit, 13-17.

14 Le Donne op cit, 274.

15 Stratta, Erica *The education of borstal boys: a study of their educational experiences prior to and during borstal training* London, Routledge and Kegan Paul, 1970 (International Library of Sociology and Social Reconstruction), 131-132.

16 Gulker op cit, 34.

17 Lutas, K M 'Strangeways Prison library' *Book trolley* 3(4) December 1971, 4.

18 Gulker op cit, 39.

19 Lutas op cit, 4.
20 Gulker op cit
21 Rubin op cit
22 Lutas op cit
23 Werner, O James 'The present legal status and conditions of prison libraries' *Law library journal* 66(3) August, 1973, 259-269.
24 MacLeod, Celeste 'Prison law libraries and you' *Library journal* 97(19) November, 1972, 3539-3545.
25 Le Donne op cit, 279.
26 Reynolds op cit, 73-91.

FIVE

LIBRARY SERVICES FOR THE ELDERLY

Introduction
THE YEARS since the end of the Second World War have
seen the introduction by public libraries of new services for
elderly readers. There have been several social trends which
have influenced this development. Perhaps the most significant of these has been the rapid increase in the elderly as
a proportion of the population. This has been apparent in
virtually every industrialised country. It has served to
emphasise the need for an appraisal of the economic and
social circumstances of the older citizen.

To determine the special problems which accompany the
process of growing old, surveys and studies have been made
which identified certain difficulties which the elderly are
likely to encounter. It has become apparent that if the aged
are to enjoy a standard of living comparable to the rest of
society then provision needs to be made for them, and the
past two decades have witnessed the growth of facilities and
services specifically for the elderly. Inevitably public libraries have been affected by this awareness, and in formulating a policy towards their elderly clients, will need to be
aware of the diverse nature of this section of the community.
Some older people will not consider it necessary for library
programmes to be devised specifically for them. Conversely,
those elderly people who are severely physically handicapped
to the point of being confined to their homes or their beds,
welcome library services which bring reading material to
them. The elderly who are living below the poverty line

often enjoy library programmes which bring them into contact with others.

Development of services in the USA

The interest in the possibility and the need for library programmes for the aged has been largely a development of the period after the Second World War. Public libraries in the United States have successfully introduced a variety of services for the elderly American citizen. The basic problem in formulating such programmes was a lack of knowledge of the distinct preferences and reading interests of the older members of the American society.

In an attempt to determine these needs The Adult Education Division of the American Library Association formed a Committee on Library Services to an Aging Population, and asked it to conduct an investigation into public library provision for the elderly. The response to the survey indicated that this concentrated primarily upon the supply of books to the homes of the elderly who were physically disabled.[1]

A later, more detailed survey, published in 1959, failed to identify any common approach by public libraries to the provision of services to the aged.[2,3] Some libraries were, apparently, reluctant to accept that the growing numbers of the elderly represented a separate problem. This reluctance did stem, in part, from a conviction that it would be wrong to treat the elderly as a distinctive section of the community. There was a concern, too, that the introduction of programmes for the elderly would result in the library offering facilities which would encroach upon the work of other agencies, particularly the social services.

The ALA did not share the conviction, held by many public librarians, that separate provision for the elderly was unnecessary. In 1959 it held a conference devoted entirely to the subject of library services to the aging. In the same year it published a reading list of books and other material: *Service to the aging* as a part of this campaign to persuade

100

librarians that there was a clear need for properly devised library facilities for older readers. The work was strengthened by the growing concern of the federal administration with the difficulties of the aged. The first White House Conference on the Aging was held in 1961. This provided a climate of official approval for the subsequent development by community agencies, including public libraries, of new opportunities for the elderly citizen.

Further impetus for the development of library programmes for the aged was given by the federal government by the financial assistance available through the Library Services and Construction Act of 1964 and, to a lesser extent, by the Older Americans Act of 1965. These federal enactments encouraged libraries to concentrate upon the provision of books and related materials rather than upon semi-educational programmes which had a limited relevance to the purpose of the library. In addition, libraries began to introduce services for the elderly confined to their homes. Large print books had an obvious relevance to the elderly, many of whom suffered from defective vision, and this form of reading material was also made available as part of the additional provision being made for the aged. Unquestionably, the availability of federal assistance was a significant factor in this sudden upsurge of interest in the elderly.

As an example of the type of programme being formulated by public libraries during this period, the work being undertaken by St Louis Public Library is not untypical. With the help of a three year federal grant, St Louis introduced a library service for the elderly who were physically disabled. The project concentrated upon taking books to the housebound elderly living in housing projects, private homes and institutions.[4] Programmes developed in other parts of the United States similarly concentrated upon reaching the elderly who could not come to the library.

The majority of the money which public libraries received for this work was made available through the provision of the Library Services and Construction Act. Henry Drennan has argued that the opportunities presented by the Older Americans Act were largely overlooked by librarians in the United States. An amendment to the act, 'Older Readers' Services', authorised the use of federal aid for a variety of library purposes, but little of this had been appropriated.[5]

Drennan suggests that this is consistent with the attitude of American public librarians towards library services for the elderly. He draws attention to the small number of public libraries which specifically budget for older reader programmes. He also observes that prior to 1966 no state library actually reported any special financial allocation for library services to the aged.[6]

In condemning this situation Drennan expresses the opinion that the elderly are entitled to the same attention and the same quality of library service as the young.[7] The reality is that the elderly have not attracted the same concern shown by librarians for their younger patrons. This in spite of the steady increase in the number of elderly people in the community. Drennan quotes the results of a survey designed to evaluate the impact of the Library Services and Construction Act upon the elderly. This showed that over two thirds of the elderly taking part in the survey approved of the new facilities and services being introduced by public libraries for them.[8] Drennan strongly advocates that public librarians should make themselves more aware of the possibilities of helping the elderly. This would entail making opportunities available for the elderly to take part in programmes for self-development. This may consist of helping the elderly to develop new interests or the library could make special provision for those wishing to start second careers. The library in doing this should be aware of the courses developed by community colleges for the elderly.[9]

Drennan expresses a conviction that the elderly are not always occupied with survival issues. With their often considerable vocabulary and their capacity for rational thought they will respond to those library programmes which extend their horizons.[10]

Although Drennan was highly critical of the apparent lack of commitment of American librarians to the needs of the elderly readers the indications are that many public libraries were making some provision at least. A survey, sponsored by the US Office of Education in 1972 revealed that the majority of public libraries were acknowledging that the elderly would benefit from services designed to meet their special requirements.[11] Eighty per cent of the public libraries responding to the enquiry reported the existence of facilities specifically for elderly readers, with over sixty per cent reaching those unable to come to the library. Libraries were providing books to the homes of the housebound elderly, depositing collections of books in old peoples' homes and making collections of large print and talking books available for the visually handicapped.

The basic difficulty, which was apparently preventing any further extension of these services, was the lack of financial resources. Less than one per cent of the total state library budget in the US was being devoted to library provision for the elderly and the physically handicapped. A high proportion of the funds which were available had come from the federal government and other sources.[12]

Developments in the UK

Many of Drennan's strictures of the American public library provision for the elderly would be equally applicable to the British equivalent. Generally the development of special library services for the elderly has lagged behind the progress made in the United States. For the most part, British public libraries have concentrated upon the reading needs of the elderly who are disabled. This has meant the introduction of housebound reader services, the formation of collections of large print books and, more recently, making library buildings more accessible for the physically handicapped.

There are reasons for the slow development of British public library services for the elderly. There has not been the

103

level of central government participation in making special facilities available. Many British librarians share the opinion, expressed by a number of their American colleagues, that the elderly do not wish to be treated as a distinct section of the community. There are less tangible reasons, which may be inherent in the differences in the clientele which the public libraries in the two countries serve. Certainly, in both the traditional public library user is drawn from the middle-class (the 'white collar worker'), but in the United States, a higher proportion of these are self-employed than in Britain. It may be that the individual who has been self-employed will be more likely to consider programmes of self development leading to a second career, than someone who has been a member of a public service and who is now in receipt of a reasonable pension.

The American public library can, perhaps, be more confident of offering or participating in courses designed to help those of retirement age who are contemplating the possibilities of embarking upon a new career. The probability is that the elderly in the United Kingdom would not respond to any programmes offered by public libraries which were designed to fit them for future employment. British librarians may feel that their limited resources are best directed towards helping those elderly who are physically disabled. This would include those who would like to use the library services, but are prevented from doing so by some disability from either coming to the library or using its resources. Any other provision for the disabled would be regarded with suspicion by many British public librarians. They would consider many of the innovations in services to the elderly undertaken by US public libraries to be outside the province of librarians and more properly the responsibility of other agencies. British librarians would further argue that the elderly themselves would resent any attempts to persuade or cajole them into participating in educational and other programmes designed to further their 'self-improvement.'

The possibilities for adapting and expanding the public library to meet the special needs and problems of the elderly

104

have been widely explored in recent years. Certain aspects of this work, namely the provision of services to the house-bound, the adaptation of library buildings and the assembly of collections of material for the visually handicapped will be considered under these headings. Those library facilities intended specifically for the elderly can be summarised as follows:

i) The provision of collections of reading material of special interest.

ii) Designating an area in the library specifically for the use of the elderly patron.

iii) Compiling booklists devoted to topics appropriate to the needs and concerns of the elderly.

iv) Acting as an information and referral centre for enquiries about social welfare, pensions, rents and other civic rights.

v) Providing programmes of events and activities of direct relevance to the needs of the elderly.

vi) Enabling local organisations for the elderly to hold exhibitions in the library of art or handicrafts produced by their members.

vii) Forming clubs and discussion groups for the aged.

viii) Introducing educational programmes for the older resident.

ix) Providing opportunities for the employment of the retired in the library in a paid or voluntary capacity.

x) Recording the reminiscences of older residents of the locality for inclusion in the local history collections.

Collections and special areas for the elderly

The book-stock of public libraries will naturally contain material which will be of special interest to the older reader. Books and magazines dealing with health, income and retirement are examples of this type of material. Some public libraries, notably those in the USA, have assembled books and periodicals of this type in special collections for the older reader. In some American libraries these collections have been housed in a defined area of the library with an appropriate caption: 'Your Leisure Years', 'Retirement

Bonanza', or other headings to indicate the scope and purpose of the collection. The response of the elderly to the provision of collections of this kind has been guarded. In some libraries the material provided has been well-used; in other libraries the response has been disappointing.

The public librarian has to be sensitive to the feelings of the older person. The onset of old age does not necessarily bring different reading interests: the books which attract the elderly are not dissimilar from those borrowed by the rest of the adult community. To imply, by the provision of special collections, that the elderly are in a separate category, is a negation of the democratic ideals of the public library.

However the librarian must also recognise that the older person may have certain preferences, which they are entitled to expect will be considered. For example, the elderly patron of a busy public library may find the bustle and noise a distraction. They might welcome the haven which a special area for the elderly will represent: this can be a place where they can browse amongst well-loved books and select from material chosen with their special interests in mind. The librarian may need to adopt an empirical approach. If the number of elderly users of the library warrants such provision and if there is an expressed demand, then the librarian should examine the desirability of a separate elderly reader collection.

There will be potential difficulties. Other users may resent being denied access to a section of the library. It may be difficult to define who is entitled to use the collection. In practice, the librarian would be wise to indicate that, while the area of the library set aside for the elderly is intended predominantly for their use, there will be no fundamental objection to other members of the library consulting the material which it contains.

The books assembled in the collection for the elderly will reflect the expressed interests of the older users of the library. Basically those books which are likely to appeal to those of advanced years: established authors of the past, works covering historical events, famous personnages of earlier periods are all likely to attract the elderly readers (see pages 113-5). The collection can also contain books and other material relevant to the problems of growing old, including official leaflets explaining the rights and benefits to which the elderly are entitled. A bulletin board placed in a prominent place in the elderly readers' area can be used to display items of current interest to the elderly: programmes introduced by other agencies for them, changes in social security and pension provision are obvious examples.

If a decision is reached to provide a separate collection of material for the elderly, it is essential that such a collection be properly supported. Any public library introducing services for the elderly reader should explore the possibilities of funding from government and other sources. In a number of countries there are provisions made for such support. The assistance provided by the federal government in the US has already been mentioned. In the UK library projects for the elderly may be eligible for grants through the urban aid programme.

A member of the staff of the public library should be given direct responsibility for any collections of reading material for the elderly. The person chosen should be familiar with the differing interests of the older reader. They should also be capable of dealing with enquiries which the elderly might make, be this an enquiry on matters relating to social welfare or for a novelist no longer in print.

Book-lists for the elderly

Reading lists can be an effective method of demonstrating the range of books and other materials available to members of the library. This technique for exploiting the bookstock can be used to draw the attention of the older to reading material likely to be of interest to them. This may, in fact, be a more suitable alternative to physically separating this material to form a collection apart, and the subjects covered in the reading lists would cover the same topics. Booklists

of the works of novelists and other imaginative writers popular with the older reader could also be produced indicating
the library's holdings of these authors.

Information services for the elderly

Many of the issues affecting the elderly require that they
have access to those official publications, issued by central
and local government departments, which explain their
rights and detail the financial and other benefits to which
they are entitled. The volume of this literature is now considerable and the phraseology in which it is couched can be
confusing.

The degree of uncertainty from which the elderly suffer
can be calculated by the benefits which remain unclaimed
each year. Sometimes this is the result of pride, but more
frequently through ignorance, or an inability to grasp the
complex regulations which govern the award of social security payments.

Although public libraries do collect and display the publications of government departments and other agencies which
relate to the elderly, the information which these documents
contain is rarely properly exploited. Ideally a professional
member of the library staff should be given responsibility
for the collection and organisation of those official and other
publications which detail not only the rights of the aged, but
also other economically deprived sections of the community.
Central and local government departments and other agencies
concerned with social welfares should be regularly circularised
requesting explanatory leaflets and other relevant publications. The material received should be prominently displayed
and fully catalogued. Those responsible for this collection
should be given the opportunity of examining the literature
regularly and familiarising themselves with any changes in
benefits, so they are in a position to advise enquirers.

Lists should be maintained of organisations both national
and local who supply information on benefits and services
to the aged. If the library is unable to answer any enquiry by

an older person on the facilities available to them, the enquiry can be referred to the appropriate agency.

It may seem, in undertaking this work, that the public library is usurping the functions of other organisations. In reply, it could be argued that the elderly are not receiving the help and information they need to claim the benefits which are rightfully theirs. Public libraries are by tradition sources of information; librarians have the expertise to collect and display publications of all types; they have the experience to disseminate the knowledge which they contain. It is a natural function of the public library service to provide the elderly with the facts they need in order to enjoy a reasonable existence.

Extension activities for the elderly

The provision of a programme of activities in the library for the elderly should be subject to the same considerations which are applied to any separate service for one category of readers. Are the interests of the older reader so different that such a range of activities is necessary? The answer must be that the elderly will, in most cases, enjoy the same lectures, musical evenings, films and other presentations which attract the entire adult community. There will, nevertheless, be the rider that there are some areas of concern that are of predominant interest to those in the older age groups, which the library can examine through lectures and other events.

There are two possible ways in which the librarian can introduce such topics for the elderly. They can be included in the general programme of lectures and talks which the library is arranging, or the library can embark upon a separate series of events for the older citizen. Whichever approach is adopted, the librarian can invite experts to deliver lectures on matters that are specifically relevant to the problems of the older person: health and nutrition, retirement and leisure, living alone, pensions and budgetary problems, social security and benefits. Such events, in addition to providing the elderly with useful information, will also give them the opportunity to meet others of their own age, perhaps to form new friendships.

Exhibitions

The public library can, on an arranged basis, make its display facilities available to old peoples' clubs and other organisations for the elderly. They can show the results of any art work or handicraft activities which they have undertaken. The display of such material will, in addition to giving pleasure to those who have created the exhibits, also publicise the contribution which local organisations are making to the welfare of the elderly. If the items displayed are available for purchase, exhibitions of this kind can be a means of raising funds for clubs and organisations for the elderly.

Clubs and discussion groups for the aged

Several public libraries in the United States have, with varying degrees of success, organised clubs and discussion groups for the elderly. The public library service of Cleveland was a pioneer in this field. As early as 1943, it had begun to develop educational and recreational facilities for the aged. In 1946 the 'Live Long and Like It Club' was formed. Cleveland also received a grant for work with the elderly from the Fund for Adult Education. This was used to introduce a programme of weekly discussion groups for the elderly which ranged over a wide selection of topics. A travel group was formed using such aids as films, books and music to supplement the talks and discussions.[13]

The work being undertaken by Cleveland acted as a stimulus for other public libraries. In 1950 the Boston Public Library formed the first 'Never too late' group for the elderly. This was sufficiently successful to encourage the formation of other 'Never too late' groups in the Boston branch libraries.[14] American public libraries began to introduce their own clubs for the elderly at which discussions on books, current affairs and other subjects took place.

110

The response of the elderly to facilities of this kind was mixed. There were reports by some libraries that they were reluctant to participate in the discussions and debates. In other cases the clubs were successful and were well-supported. The reasons for the lack of response in some localities are difficult to identify. It is possible that older people are reluctant to participate in activities which differentiate them from the rest of the community. Again, the elderly do not form a homogeneous group: their interests, beliefs, their social and education backgrounds will vary widely; the responses of men and women of sixty-five will often differ from those who are ten or fifteen years older. The group leader will need to exercise considerable skill in taking these factors into consideration when leading the debate.

Further education for the elderly

Jean Brooks has provided an account of the work of the Dallas Public Library where a demanding programme of self-education for the elderly was introduced in the 1970s. Here the library provided study facilities which were linked to the college level examination program. Guides to study were produced and reading lists on twenty different subjects were prepared by the faculty of the Southern Methodist University. Five of the Dallas Public Library branches acted as centres for older persons who wished to study for the college level examinations or for those who only wanted to pursue the courses for 'self-enrichment'.[15]

The benefits for the elderly who embarked upon these educational programmes are, Brooks suggests, the acquisition of new interests and fresh knowledge. They can help, too, to narrow the gap between generations. She recognises that the elderly will face special problems: they may suffer from an inability to remember facts, there will be difficulties caused by faulty eyesight or impaired hearing, they will tend to tire if compelled to sit for lengthy periods. Moreover, there may be a reluctance to venture out for classes held in the evenings, and a disinclination to expose one's character before new

111

acquaintances, with the implied threat of competition (fears which are not necessarily confined to the elderly).

In conclusion, Brooks does cite the results of research studies which suggest that older persons who continue their education enjoy better health, increased happiness and often have a greater sense of self esteem than those who do not pursue such programmes.

While it is possible to accept this, it is also reasonable to question whether public libraries are the proper agencies for providing discussion groups and further education programmes for the elderly. A personal view is that activities of this kind are not the legitimate concern of the public library. The majority of librarians lack the experience and the necessary training to undertake work of this kind. It may be, in some communities, that the public library is the only institution with the accommodation and the facilities for holding meetings and other functions. In these circumstances, the public library can make its facilities available for group activities for the elderly but again it may be better that the organisation of meetings and other events should be undertaken by those familiar with work with the elderly. In normal circumstances it is more fitting that the public library leaves the provision of educational and other 'self-development' opportunities for the older person to community colleges, community centres and clubs for the elderly.

Employing the elderly in libraries

The difficulties which the elderly may experience on retirement after leading busy and full lives are evident. Some welcome the opportunity to enter new fields of employment; it can represent an extra source of income and a means of gaining new interests, new friends and acquaintances. The public library might consider employing retired people in those areas where their experience and knowledge will be of value. Their assistance can be especially useful in serving housebound readers, and their advice could be sought in planning any extension programmes for the elderly.

The retired person can be recruited as a paid assistant or may be engaged as a voluntary worker. There are potential difficulties in employing the elderly: during times of economic recession and high unemployment trade unions may feel that the work should be left to the paid staff. Also, the elderly may find some aspects of library work tiring and may, in some cases, be more prone to making mistakes. In spite of the difficulties the older person still has something to offer the community and public at large, and public and other types of library may feel they have a duty to provide opportunities for the elderly.

Local knowledge and the elderly

The local history department of the public library may be able to augment the information they have on the locality by persuading those who have been resident in the area for a long period to come along and talk about their early memories. If these recollections are taped, the library will be able to build up a unique record of local history.

Older persons can often be persuaded to donate or bequeath their old photographs, prints and other material to the library. As well as enhancing the local history collections, they enjoy talking about their memories and it gives them the feeling that their past life is of interest and worthy of being placed on record.

The reading tastes of the elderly

There are few studies based upon scientific principles which show ways in which the reading tastes of the elderly differ or coincide with the rest of the adult community. Very little is known of the changes which take place in people's reading habits as they grow older or indeed whether they do change significantly.

The results of a survey conducted into the reading habits of a group of US Army veterans in 1970 is not perhaps applicable to the reading tastes of all elderly people.[16] Those taking part in the survey were all men with extensive military experience, living in institutionalised conditions. However, the survey suggested that elderly gentlemen did have certain reading preferences which were relevant only to them. There was a preference for biographical material, particularly for the lives of prominent figures contemporary with themselves. Books on aspects of the past were popular: old-time radio, silent pictures, famous stage shows, vintage cars, steamships and historical railways were amongst those subjects attracting interest.

There was an eagerness to read material which brought back memories: verse was sought after, especially those poems which were read and learnt at school (with the names of Longfellow, Kipling, Tennyson and Service being frequently mentioned). The same attitude was revealed in the choice of fiction, and some established authors were clearly regarded as old friends with, for example, the novels of Yerby, Slaughter and Edgar Rice Burroughs being constantly requested.

Those taking part in the survey had their marked dislikes. There was a strong aversion to books which portrayed contemporary violence and novels depicting sexual themes in frank terms. Current affairs magazines attracted little interest, and apart from reading newspapers and magazines the elderly were indifferent to social issues. This lack of interest in events in the world may be part of the withdrawal from life which is often part of the process of growing old.

Public librarians in the United Kingdom who have developed special services for the elderly have noted some aspects of the reading patterns of those being reached by these facilities. In general, while the elderly do have certain preferences and prejudices, the books which they choose hardly reveal any sharp divergence from the reading habits of the rest of the community. Older readers being served by the Aberdeen housebound reader services reveals that older women had a preference for romances and family stories but disliked books which contained explicit sexual references. Elderly men being reached by the service liked non-fiction but those who read novels preferred western and mystery stories.[17] This indicates that the reading needs of the elderly will often mirror that of the younger members of the community. Clearly, research into this aspect of library provision is urgently needed. Similarly, librarians would welcome information on whether people read more or less as they grow older.

The lack of documented research into the reading patterns of the elderly does compel librarians to formulate special programmes for the aged on the basis of their own experience. Public libraries which have initiated such activities have found that generally the elderly welcome the availability of services intended specifically for them. However, a successful event provided by one public library does not necessarily mean that a similar programme in another community will automatically meet with the same favourable response. Librarians who are working with the older members of the library will need to recognise that they are serving a section of society whose needs, wishes and attitudes are as diverse as the entire adult community.

REFERENCES
1 Phinney, Eleanor 'Library services to an aging population; report on a post-card survey' *ALA bulletin* 51(8) September 1957, 607-609.

2 Phinney, Eleanor 'Trends in library services to the aging' *ALA bulletin* 53(6) June 1959, 534-535.

3 Phinney, Eleanor *A study of current practices in public library service to the aging: an evaluative report* University of Illinois, Graduate School of Library Science Occasional paper no 6. Champaign-Urbana, 1961. Cited in Javelin, Muriel C 'How library service to the aging has developed' *Library trends* 21(3) January 1973, 371.

4 Brown, Eleanor Frances *Library services to the disadvantaged* Metuchen (NJ), Scarecrow Press, 1971, 314.

5 Drennan, Henry T 'Library legislation discovered' *Library trends* 24(1) July, 1975, 120.

6 Ibid 121.

7 Ibid 123.

8 Ibid 121-2.

9 Ibid 123.

10 Ibid 123-4.

11 *National survey of library services to the aging* Phase 2 Final Report. Cleveland Public Library (US Department of Health, Education and Welfare. Office of Education Bureau of Libraries and Educational Technology, 1972.)

12 Drennan op cit, 120.

13 Long, Fern 'The live long and like it club—the Cleveland Public Library' *Library trends* 17(1) July 1968, 68-71.

14 Javelin, Muriel C op cit, 367-368.

15 Brooks, Jean S 'Older persons and the college-level examination program' *AHIL quarterly* 12(2/3) spring/summer 1972, 17-18.

16 Buswell, Christina H 'Our other customers: reading and the aged' *Wilson Library bulletin* 45(5) January 1971, 467-476.

17 Critchley, W E 'Library services for housebound readers in Scotland' *Book trolley* 2(3) September 1968, 56.

SIX

LIBRARY SERVICES FOR THE DISABLED

The disabled in the community
THE ADVANCES made by medical science which have affected the number of elderly people in the modern community have also contributed to the rise in the proportion of physically disabled persons in society. There are many individuals alive who would have died but for the availability of modern medical knowledge and drugs. The more fortunate may be enabled to return to society to live normal lives; for others there can be severe restrictions placed upon mobility and free intercourse with the rest of society.

The degree of incapacity which the physically handicapped suffer varies considerably. Even those afflicted by the same complaint differ widely in their reactions. Some illnesses have long periods of remission which enable the sufferer to lead a comparatively full life, if sporadically. Others are progressive, with those afflicted having to accept an increasing reduction in their physical powers. There are those who suffer from more than one disability. And amongst all these individuals, some will be determined to overcome, as far as possible, the restrictions imposed on them, whilst others reconcile themselves to a circumscribed existence.

The public librarian contemplating the introduction of special services for the disabled will need to be conscious of the widely different effect of certain illnesses and physical conditions. Other considerations are principally those related to the number and distribution of the disabled.

The librarian will recognise that, as with the elderly, the majority of physically handicapped people are able to lead a life which is only partially restricted by their disability. In the United Kingdom, for example, it is estimated that three quarters of those classified as physically disabled are able to go out unaccompanied without experiencing any real difficulty.[1] Only one per cent, the majority of these women, are actually confined permanently to their beds, although a further two per cent are 'chairfast'.[2] Two per cent of those who are unable to leave their homes are women over the age of seventy-five. In fact almost eighty per cent of those permanently housebound (the equivalent American terms are 'homebound' or 'shut-ins') are women, only six per cent of these being under the age of fifty.[3]

The comparable figures for men carry further implications for the librarian contemplating the introduction of a service to housebound readers. Only two per cent of the housebound are men under the age of fifty.[4] This means that the majority of those needing books delivered to their homes will be, in the average community, elderly women.

The development of public library services to the disabled has been influenced by the recognition by governments in a number of countries that there is a need to help those who are severely physically handicapped. The emergence of state-aided programmes is typified by events which have taken place in the United Kingdom. A number of parliamentary enactments to assist the disabled culminated in 1970 with the introduction of the Chronically Sick and Disabled Persons Act, which enabled local authorities to introduce a wide spectrum of services for the handicapped.

The act contains clauses which are of direct relevance to public libraries. Local authorities are instructed to fulfil the following obligations:

i) The provision . . . or assistance . . . in obtaining wireless, television, library or similar recreational facilities . . .

ii) The provision of lectures, games, outings and other recreational facilities outside his home, or assistance . . . in taking advantage of educational facilities. . .

iii) . . . the provision of facilities for, or assistance in, travelling to and from his home for the purpose of participating in any service provided under arrangements made by the authority.

iv) Any person undertaking the provision of any building or premises to which the public are admitted, whether on payment or otherwise, shall, in the means of access both to and within the building or premises, and in the parking facilities and sanitary conveniences to be available (if any), make provision, in so far as it is, in the circumstances, both practicable and reasonable, for the needs of the members of the public visiting the building or premises who are disabled.

Many libraries in Britain have responded to the letter and spirit of these provisions, and many social service departments are providing essential services to those who are physically disabled. This includes help in the home with domestic chores, the supply of ready-cooked meals as well as regular visits by social and medical workers. The development of housebound reader services is just one facet of this trend.

The public library service, in formulating programmes for the handicapped, needs to keep in mind the fact that many young disabled persons, given the right assistance, are capable of leading satisfying and productive lives. Rehabilitation courses can offset the disadvantages imposed by physical condition. This does not minimise the value of library services to those confined to their homes, for those who are bedridden will need a supply of reading material to relieve the frustration and the boredom which they inevitably suffer. Unable to leave their homes, such individuals frequently lead a lonely existence, deprived of many of the pleasures which the rest of the community enjoy. The introduction of library services, which have taken reading material into their homes, has been one of the major humanitarian achievements of the public library since the Second World War.

Planning a library service

There are certain characteristics quickly apparent about the housebound: they are likely to be female, of retirement age, and living in social isolation. In many cases they will

119

also be suffering from economic deprivation and will be dependent upon a pension or social benefits for their income.

These characteristics are not, of course, applicable to every housebound person. The librarian planning a library service to the physically disabled will need to be aware of the diverse nature of the group he is attempting to reach. There are two basic divisions: those confined to their homes and those living in institutions.

These categories can be further subdivided:

i) The permanently housebound. This can be a misleading description—there will be those compelled to remain permanently in bed, some are simply restricted to a wheelchair. The majority, however, are able to move about their homes to a limited extent, and a minority will be able to leave their homes for a limited period.

ii) The permanently housebound child. This includes children confined to their homes for physical or psychological reasons. They may have been badly malformed at birth, or severely mentally handicapped. Some may be receiving education in their own homes.

iii) The temporarily housebound. This comprises individuals compelled to remain at home whilst recovering from injury or illness. It is possible that some of those temporarily incapacitated may eventually become permanently housebound.

iv) The permanently institutionalised. Those who are living in old people's homes and establishments for the severely mentally retarded and the chronically ill.

v) The temporarily institutionalised. This embraces those receiving instruction in rehabilitation centres, or in residential schools for the blind and the deaf. It can also include those in nursing homes recovering from a severe illness.

The first step for a public library which is intending to introduce a housebound reader service to make is to establish the number and whereabouts of those needing books supplied to their homes. In the UK a reasonable starting point will be the registers of the disabled which local authorities

120

are required to keep. These are often badly compiled, inadequate and incomplete, but they can be a valuable aid in making an initial assessment of the potential demand. Another source of information will be social service departments which are already providing services of various kinds to the disabled, though officials may decline on the grounds of confidentiality to supply the names and addresses of those suffering from certain illnesses. Voluntary organisations engaged in work with the disabled should be able to supply information on those who might welcome a supply of books. Religious bodies, family doctors, even members of the general public may be able to help the library gather the necessary data on the disabled and the housebound in the area.

In Britain the public library service may also be able to arrive at a reasonably accurate assessment of the possible number of housebound persons in the locality by using a formula based upon a survey published in 1971 by the Social Services Division of the Office of Population Censuses and Surveys. The survey revealed that one man in every one hundred would be likely to be disabled in the age group sixteen to twenty-nine; for those between the ages of thirty to forty-nine the figure would be three in one hundred, with the figures for women being slightly lower in each case.[5] The number of disabled amongst those over the age of fifty does increase dramatically, with one in twelve of those men and women aged between fifty and sixty-four having some degree of physical impairment.[6]

The existence of a number of housebound people in the area does not necessarily mean that all will necessarily require books. Some will have family, friends or voluntary workers already collecting books for them. Others will not require books, either because they have never habitually read, or because the nature of their complaint makes it difficult to handle or to read printed material.

A member of the library staff will have to visit every *possible* user of a housebound reader service. Ideally, such a service will be under the direct control of a professional librarian and, again ideally, the person to assume responsibility for the initial house calls will be appointed during the planning stage. The preliminary visits will be used to obtain essential information: reading tastes, educational backgrounds, and the nature of the physical disability. Further information can be gathered on special reading problems. Will the reader require large print books? Are there any difficulties in handling books? Is the disabled person a member of an ethnic minority group requiring books in a language other than English? At this stage an index of readers, noting relevant details, should be put into operation.

If the demand for a housebound reader service is considerable it may not be possible to serve everyone immediately. In these circumstances, the librarian has to determine priority. Factors to be taken into consideration include the individual's need for reading material, their degree of physical disability and the availability of relatives and friends to collect books.

Liaison with the wardens of local institutions for the disabled will be necessary to ascertain if a service is needed in each, and to decide how best the requirements of each establishment might be met. The librarian will need to know the number of people in the institution, their average age and the numbers of each sex. It would also be useful to know if any member of the institution would be willing to assume responsibility for the library service and if suitable accommodation for displaying the books would be available.

Staffing

It was suggested earlier that control of the service should preferably be invested in a professionally qualified librarian. This ideal has been rarely achieved in the United Kingdom, where public libraries rely heavily upon the assistance of voluntary workers. In some cases the housebound reader service is virtually under the control of a voluntary organisation. In the UK this is often the Women's Royal Voluntary Service (WRVS), the library's contribution being confined to the supply of reading material. Economic factors have contributed to this situation: public libraries have been unable to meet the additional costs of supplying a service to readers' homes from their own resources. But there is, also, a widely-held view that housebound reader services have a strong affinity with social work. Volunteers, therefore, are more likely to possess the necessary qualities of tact, humility and patience than professional library staff.

This argument will be examined later. Sufficient to say now that the past decade has seen a gradual recognition that professional librarians do much to make library services to the housebound more effective; this without any loss of sympathy for the plight of the disabled.

The following duties would be appropriately the responsibility of a professional librarian:

i) The initial organisation of the service, identifying the different categories of reader. The librarian needs to make frequent follow-up visits to ensure that the reading material being delivered is appropriate to the individual reader's needs.

ii) The selection of book-stock.

iii) The planning of routes in order to ensure that each housebound reader receives a regular and adequate supply of books.

iv) Publicising the service: giving talks to clubs for the disabled, welfare centres and homes for the disabled.

v) Liaising with official and voluntary bodies concerned with services to the disabled and the elderly.

vi) The general administration of the service: planning for future growth, preparing the necessary financial estimates, monitoring current expenditure.

Some public libraries in the United Kingdom have linked the post of librarian of the housebound reader service with responsibility for supervising hospital patient libraries. There are some advantages, perhaps the most significant being that the supply of library facilities to the sick and the disabled will be coordinated. For a public library serving a small community, this is a way of justifying the appointment of a professional librarian for administering library services to the housebound and those in hospital. However in a large authority, the librarian assuming responsibility for hospital as well as housebound reader services will need adequate professional and non-professional support staff if the service is to be comprehensive for both groups of readers.

In general, the same arguments for and against employing voluntary staff in hospital libraries will be relevant to the recruitment of volunteers for the housebound reader service. The Aves Report (1969) contains some illuminating statements made by voluntary workers, who generally considered themselves more friendly and approachable than the officials engaged in the same field.[7] There is a widely-held opinion that salaried staff are less anxious to establish good relations with those they are paid to serve, and this has considerable implications. Those who are restricted to their homes all day regard the arrival of the housebound reader service as something of a social occasion. They will expect the person bringing their books to stay and talk, and conversation will not necessarily be confined to the books being exchanged. Voluntary workers, it has been argued, are more likely to have the relaxed approach necessary to gain the confidence of those they are visiting. If the volunteers are recruited from retired persons, they will often be nearer the age group of the housebound.

Much of this is speculation and, as W E Critchley has cogently stated, the housebound reader service is, above all, a library service and not part of the social services.[8] Non-professional library assistants can bring their experience and training to meet the special needs of the disabled and the elderly. This means that the housebound reader service staffed by full-time salaried workers will be more efficient than one which is provided by amateur volunteers, however well-meaning they may be. Nor are qualities of patience, tact and tolerance the sole prerogatives of voluntary workers. If the non-professional staff selected are carefully vetted, then there is no reason why those to be visited should not receive a library service with pleasure, even while recognising that there is an obligation on the service to make each visit.

There may occasionally be difficulties in finding non-professional staff who have the right qualities to make successful members of the housebound reader service. It may mean taking experienced staff away from other areas of the library service. As many public libraries suffer from a shortage of older assistants, it may be that younger members of staff will have to work in a service which is reaching predominantly older people. This may well be an advantage, as W E Critchley reports, the young assistant, sometimes only sixteen years of age, is quite capable of working with '. . . zest, sympathy and cheerfulness . . .'[9]

A successful compromise between the fully professional and the all-voluntary service, as tried by a number of public libraries, is to have the housebound reader service directed by a professional librarian with a volunteer staff helping with the visits to the homes of the disabled. Furthermore, it has to be acknowledged that during periods of economic recession, public libraries may not have the staff, the facilities or the resources to give a properly-organised supply of reading material to those unable to visit the library. A service to the housebound which is heavily reliant upon voluntary assistance is better than no service at all. It is, however, a sad commentary upon the priorities of society that a public library budget should not automatically include financial provision for disabled readers.

Materials

Some libraries operating a service to the housebound have built a separate stock of books based upon the known reading interests of those being visited. There are certain administrative benefits, and it does obviate the problem of removing popular works from the main stock of the library for a lengthy period, but such a collection will be expensive to maintain. It also needs to be changed frequently if it is to give the housebound reader a good choice.

A number of successful housebound reader services draw upon the existing resources of the public library, and this can cause difficulties if the works being taken on the rounds are also required by readers at the library. The resentment which this might cause strengthens the case for a separate stock of books specifically for the housebound readers.

A satisfactory compromise is to assemble a collection of popular works which will satisfy the majority of those being visited, with the requests for the more specialist subjects being met from the main stock of the library. The experience of housebound readers' services does indicate that there will be requests for a wide range of books. The Aberdeen Public Library received enquiries for musical scores, language tutors, art books, and career guides from those being visited.[10] Young housebound readers may be pursuing courses of study, either to fit them for employment or personal interest. There may be students or school children who have been temporarily or permanently prevented by accident or illness from attending their schools, colleges or universities. The housebound service can, perhaps, obtain the necessary reading material for the disabled student. Children who are physically handicapped, in addition to receiving a supply of recreational reading material through the housebound reader service, may also need books to supplement lessons they are being given in their own homes.

Delivery and route planning

The experience of many libraries is that a vehicle can be permanently employed in the delivery of books. One British public library found that when the number of persons needing a housebound reader service exceeded two hundred, a second vehicle was needed.

If the vehicle used is specially designed for its job there will naturally be an improvement in speed and ease of service. It needs to be large enough to carry all the books to be delivered on one round. The assumption is that readers will not usually enter the vehicle to choose their books and it will not therefore be necessary, as in the case of a mobile library, to allow for the free movement of the public. The roof of the van must be sufficiently high to enable staff to enter and collect books with ease, and the vehicle should be wide enough to allow for shelves to be fitted on each side (although not so wide as to make it difficult to maneouvre in narrow streets). Shelves should be deep enough to house the consignments of books for each visit.

When there is no vehicle available, a number of alternative arrangements for book delivery can be made. One possibility is to use the mobile library, which has the advantage of carrying a comparatively generous range of books from which a choice can be made. But the use of a mobile library in this way can present practical difficulties: it is large and cumbersome for urban use, and readers may feel that the appearance of a large vehicle at their homes will advertise their condition to others. The mobile library can be used to better effect in visiting institutions, where ambulant residents will be able to browse in the book collection and select both for themselves and other residents.

Another possibility is to pay members of the library staff an allowance to use their own cars to deliver books to the housebound. Similarly, volunteers may be willing to use their own vehicles for transporting books. In fact voluntary organisations have often acquired their own vehicles for the provision of services to the handicapped, and are often prepared to make this transport available for book delivery to the disabled.

These are alternatives which are inevitably far less effective than the use of a vehicle which has been specifically designed and those libraries which do depend upon such forms of transport frequently have waiting lists of those requiring a book service to their homes.

Each reader should be visited at least once every fortnight, and the visits will need to be on the same day and approximately the same time. Elderly people in particular value the reassurance which a pattern of regular visits can bring. The majority of calls will be made during the day. In 1966, Wandsworth Public Library was compelled by the pressure on their housebound reader service to make some visits in the evenings.[11] Ultimately this was found to be unsatisfactory and added another vehicle to the service, enabling deliveries to be made during the day.[12]

There are several factors which influence the number of visits that can be made in one day, and there is a wide variation in the experience of the optimum number of calls a service can achieve. Urban areas, for instance, are easier to serve than rural ones.

Library staff must also recognise that a visit is not just a matter of delivering books. For the disabled person the arrival of the visitor from the library may be something of an occasion. The staff may want to discuss the books which were delivered on the last visit, to determine if they were suitable or not. For such reasons it might be undesirable to insist upon a strict timetable for visits, whilst recognising that the efficiency of a service depends upon the maintenance of a regular schedule of calls.

Special services

Some readers will experience difficulty in handling books, others may be unable to read printed material. One relatively common complaint is that of defective sight. Large print books will be available, and for those who are completely blind the library can assist in supplying details of agencies which makes books in braille and on tape available (see chapter seven). The housebound reader service can also act as a link between such agencies and blind people who are unable to leave their homes.

Libraries have experimented with the provision of non-book material to the elderly and the physically handicapped. As Theda Kellner has said, the elderly have 'grown-up' with electronic communication systems: radio, television, cinema,

128

gramophone and, latterly, the cassette player.[13] Many of them welcome access to non-book material, particularly recorded music on disc or tape. Other provision for the housebound by public libraries includes the loan of art reproductions, games and tapes of foreign language material.

A further possibility is to arrange reading sessions in the homes of those who are prevented by physical infirmity from reading books. The disabled often welcome the personal experience of having a book read to them, and the events and characters in the book can provide discussion points. Reading books aloud does require some skill, and a library contemplating the introduction of this facility may find that there is shortage of suitable volunteers.

Several films deal with the problems of the disabled and the elderly. Some provide information on services available to the physically handicapped and the aged, others discuss the special difficulties which these groups experience. Films of this kind can be profitably shown by the staff of the public library in the residential homes for the disabled and the elderly. This work can be supplemented by the provision of relevant printed material.

Books by post

County libraries, which have to provide for a scattered population, can reach the housebound living in remote areas by mailing books to them. This facility must be seen as a substitute for the delivery of books by road transport. The cost of sending parcels of books will be considerable; in addition to the postal charges there is also the considerable staff time used in selecting and despatching material. The readers will not have the benefit of regular contact with library staff, who will have to rely upon letter or telephone to establish the reader's needs. Nevertheless, for the disabled reader outside the reach of the regular library service, the supply of books by post is a valuable alternative.

Deposit collections

The residents of institutions for the disabled can be provided with a library service by deposit collections of literature. The books loaned will need to be changed frequently if the collection is to retain the interest of the residents. The area available for the display of the books will often be limited and the service will usually be confined to a supply of recreational reading material. The books should be properly displayed and the public library may need to loan bookcases to the institution. The collection should, preferably, be housed in a locked room otherwise the loss rate will be intolerably high.

The warden, or one of the assistants, might be willing to act as librarian; sometimes one of the residents can be persuaded to accept this responsibility. Alternatively the housebound reader service can arrange for the home to be visited by a librarian, at a fixed time each week, to issue books. There will be advantages in having the institution visited regularly in this way. In addition to collecting requests, library staff can note how effective the collection is, whether certain books need to be withdrawn, and if certain sections of the stock needs strengthening. It will be an opportunity to liaise with the warden to determine if the service needs extending in any way. The library may consider the possibilities of offering a programme of extension activities: films, talks, gramophone record recitals and other events. These activities can be held in the institution, or transport can be arranged to take the residents to the public library.

Deposit collections can also be made at clubs and centres for the disabled and the elderly. These will include community centres for the physically handicapped and the disabled. Again, the collection needs to be properly supervised, with some member of the club or centre assuming responsibility for its administration. The public library will have to accept a high loss rate from deposit collections of this kind, and normally the institution should not be expected to meet the cost of replacing books. To insist upon recompense

130

for missing books could result in a loss of goodwill and the institution might decline to accept further responsibility for deposit collections.

Another possibility is to deposit books in blocks of flats which have been specifically designated for the disabled and the elderly. A resident may be persuaded to assume responsibility for issuing the books, with occasional visits by staff of the library.

Administration

Whether the disabled are living in their homes or in an institution, the quality of the service they are receiving is not comparable to that received by the rest of the community. The disabled reader will be denied the opportunity to range over a comprehensive collection of books. Many of the extension activities provided by the public library will be denied to the physically handicapped.

In order to compensate for the inferior library service, the administrative procedures for issuing material can be modified. Housebound readers should be allowed to borrow as many books as they need until the next visit. Requests for books should not be subject to the charge normally levied. There should not be a rigidly fixed period of loan imposed upon the housebound reader and fines should certainly not be charged for the late return of books.

Library design

The majority of those suffering from a physical disability will not be confined to their homes or an institution. In order to assist the disabled to lead as normal a life as possible, considerable thought has been given in recent years to the design of public buildings, the intention being to eliminate obstacles to the use of buildings by the physically handicapped. As part of this movement, librarians have also been examining the possibility of removing those features of their buildings which prevent the disabled from freely entering and using the collections.

One stimulus to examine the obstructions which the disabled face when trying to enter public buildings has been provided in the United Kingdom by the Chronically Sick and Disabled Persons Act of 1970, which requires that public buildings should be accessible, as far as practicable, to the disabled. Many British libraries, in response to the requirements of the act, have made substantial modifications to their buildings. The cost of redesigning a library building in order to make it more accessible might be considerable. The librarian, before proposing extensive modifications to an existing structure, needs to consider the following questions:

i) What are the limitations which different physical disabilities impose upon the disabled? How do these affect their use of the library?

ii) How many disabled persons are there in the community served by the library? What is their potential response if the building were to be adapted for their use?

iii) How many disabled persons are already members of the library? What difficulties do they experience in their use of the library's services?

iv) What will be the cost of the necessary modifications? Will such expenditure be justified by an increased use of the library by the physically handicapped?

The question of cost is clearly crucial. Unlike the hospital library, the public library is predominantly used by those who are not suffering from any disability. If the building is modified to enable the handicapped to use its resources, the work will have to be undertaken to meet the needs of a minority of users. The librarian, in devoting what could be a considerable proportion of the library budget to modify the building for the handicapped, must recognise that this is being done for a small percentage of the population to be served. It may be that a comprehensive housebound reader service will be a more effective way of reaching those who are unable to use the conventional library facilities. The two possibilities need to be carefully balanced before expensive modifications are made.

There are several categories of potential users:

i) The ambulant disabled, who can be defined as those who are permanently physically impaired. They are not compelled to use a wheelchair but find their mobility restricted. Some may be able to walk without aids, others may need recourse to sticks or crutches.

ii) Those in wheelchairs who can reach the library but who find it difficult to gain entry because of the steps to the main entrance to the building, or some other physical obstacle.

iii) Regular users of the library who are physically disabled who would welcome some modification, either to the building or the arrangement of the interior of the library or the methods used to display the stock, which would enable them to use the service more effectively. This can, for example, include the partially sighted who would benefit from improved lighting or the deaf who would find more comprehensive library guiding helpful.

The number of people in a community who would use the library if it were adapted to meet their particular disability is an important factor in reaching a decision to modify a library building. There have been a number of social changes which have increased the potential use of public libraries by the disabled. Some of these influences have already been discussed—the increasing number of elderly people in the community, for example. As the advent of old age is frequently associated with the onset of physical disability, there will, inevitably, be a growing number of elderly people in society who find it difficult to gain access to public buildings.

The availability of specially designed vehicles for the disabled has enabled many of them to reach services and facilities hitherto denied them. Similarly, improved medical treatment and modern aids for the disabled now permit even the most severely physically handicapped person some degree of mobility. Given the right circumstances the disabled should be able to make use of existing library services.

The evidence available on the use which the disabled would make of libraries if they were more accessible is not wholly conclusive. A survey conducted by Selwyn Goldsmith

133

of wheelchair users in Norwich and Taunton, did not suggest that there was an overwhelming demand for access to libraries from this section of the community.[14] It is reasonable to suppose that the disabled would make more use of public libraries if they were specially adapted to meet their needs. The librarian will, nevertheless, need to balance this possibility against the costs of such modifications and the effect this will have upon other library users.

If a library building is to be modified for the use of the severely physically handicapped, then the exterior facilities of the building will need to be surveyed. The two main areas of concern are the availability of parking facilities for the disabled, and easy access into the building.

Parking facilities:

Space should be reserved in the library car-park for the disabled who arrive in a car or disabled person's vehicle. The space allowed for the disabled wheelchair user will need to be wider than that allowed for the ambulant disabled. This will be necessary in order to permit them to move from their vehicle into the wheelchair. An ideal would be 3.60m (11 feet 10 inches) with a minimum of 3.20m (10 feet 6 inches). For the ambulant disabled to park their cars, there should be an ideal width of 3.00m (9 feet 10 inches).[15] This is based upon the assumption that the standard parking space will be 2.40m (7 feet 10 inches) in width.

The parking spaces for the disabled should be sited as near as possible to the entrance to the library. This not only reduces the distance they have to cover; it also obviates the dangers of moving behind rows of parked cars.

If the library does not have a parking area, the librarian can try to secure the agreement of the local transport authority to have certain sections of the roadway adjacent to the library reserved for the vehicles of disabled users. This may be particularly necessary in the inner city where parking may be restricted. In the UK, however, registered disabled persons do have the right to leave their vehicles where parking is normally prohibited.

The approach to the library from the car-park and the roads adjacent to the library should be as uninterrupted as possible. This is especially desirable for those in wheelchairs but it will also be helpful to the ambulant disabled. The library entrance:

A common architectural feature of older library buildings is an imposing flight of steps up to the main entrance. This represents a considerable obstacle to all those suffering from locomotory difficulties. Where such steps exist, an alternative means of access to the library should be provided. One possibility is to provide a ramp alongside the steps, and Goldsmith has provided a detailed specification for this type of construction;[16] the ramp should not be too steep and it should be wide enough to allow for the passage of wheelchairs. Goldsmith also recommends a number of safety features: a handrail is desirable, the surface should be composed of non-slip material, and, as protection against inclement weather, there should be a protective canopy. Another possibility is to have electric heating under the surface of the ramp which will be useful for melting ice or snow.

Ramps can be used by the wheelchair user, the elderly and the ambulant disabled. If, however, the slope of the ramp is steep then an alternative for the ambulant is to provide an approach with shallow steps, the steps to be not more than 16.5 cm (6½ inches) in height.[17] Should the exterior of the building not permit the construction of a ramp then another entrance should be available, this being clearly signposted.

It has been suggested that provision of ramps and separate entrances implies that the physically handicapped are in some way different from the rest of the community. The indications are that this is not a real concern to the disabled themselves.

Entrance doors should be as light as possible and the spring controlling their operation should be strong enough to ensure that it closes slowly, facilitating the passage of those with limited mobility. The use of revolving doors should be avoided whenever possible. If they have to be fitted, then an adjoining entrance with a door of conventional design should be provided. One possibility is to have an electrically operated door at the entrance to the library, which opens on approach. These are, however, expensive to install and maintenance costs may be high. Doors should be wide enough to admit wheelchair users, and Goldsmith recommends a minimum width of 75 cm (2 feet 5½ inches).[18]

The entrance to the library should be gently sloped, or a 'flexible' threshold can be installed. The foyer should be wide enough to permit wheelchairs to manoeuvre. There should also be space allocated for wheelchairs to be parked for those users who have sufficient mobility to walk about the building choosing their books.

Internal circulation

To facilitate the use of libraries by the disabled, Goldsmith has made two basic recommendations, that the main public areas should be accessible to those in wheelchairs and that the steps and stairways in those areas should be designed so that they can be used by the ambulant disabled.

If the public departments are to be adapted for the disabled, then any modifications will be a matter of compromise. If for example the bookstock was displayed so that all the items were within reach of the wheelchair user, then bookcases would need to be not more than 1.32 m (4 feet 6 inches) in height. This would considerably reduce the number of books which could be displayed for other library users. There are, therefore, practical limitations on the amount of modifications which can be made to the library. Even so, there are many possibilities for examining and adapting the ways in which the library is administered and arranged to make its services more accessible for the disabled.

The size of bookcases is one such. Goldsmith recommends that books in lending libraries should not be displayed on shelves higher than 1.50 m (4 feet 11 inches) or lower than 25 cm (9 inches). An ideal would be 1.75 m (5 feet

9 inches) in height and 38 cm (1 foot 3 inches) from the floor.[19] Goldsmith suggests that bookcases in other sections of the library will be planned with these dimensions in mind. He does add the proviso that where staff are willing to reach books for disabled readers, as part of their normal duties, then the upper and lower limits of the bookcases can be increased.[20] This seems to be a matter of staff instruction, with staff being trained to identify those who need help.

The aisles between the bookcases should be wide enough to permit a wheelchair to move freely without inconveniencing other library users. A minimum of 95 cm (3 feet) should be left within rows of bookcases which, given the sympathy which other members of the public will have for the disabled, will normally be sufficient for the disabled to choose their books with a minimum of discomfort.

The chairs, tables and other items of furniture provided for the general public are not always suitable for use by the disabled. Low chairs, for example, can cause difficulties for those who are physically handicapped. Some chairs should be made available in which the seat is at least 46 cm — 58 cm (18 — 22 inches) high, with a minimum width of 58.4 cm (23 inches) and an overall height of 1.04 m (3 feet 5 inches). The chairs should be light enough to be moved easily but at the same time they should be firm and stable, giving a natural, comfortable sitting position. Preferably some should be fitted with armrests.

Certain of the tables in the study and browsing areas should be high enough to give clearance to the arms of a wheelchair. This would enable the wheelchair user to work or read in the library. To facilitate this there should be a minimum clearance of 15.5 cm (6 inches).

Libraries, in recent years, have been making increased use of carpeting to cover the floors in public areas. The benefits are considerable: carpets absorb noise, it gives a welcoming appearance to the library, it will add to the general warmth of the building. For the disabled, carpet provides a non-slip surface and it will give some protection against the worst effects of a fall. Wheelchair users may experience some difficulty in pushing through thickly woven carpets. If there are a number of regular users of the library in wheelchairs, artificial non-woven carpets can provide a hard-wearing, relatively smooth surface for the free movement of wheelchairs. If carpet tiles are used, they will need to be firmly fixed to the floor if they are not to provide a potential hazard.

For busy libraries a more durable floor covering may be considered necessary and cork tiles can give a suitable non-slip surface. Alternatively, vinyl floor covering can be used and, if this is left unpolished, it will provide a hardwearing surface which will be relatively safe for the ambulant disabled. If the floor covering has to be polished, there are a number of anti-slip polishes which can be used.

Wherever possible, split level floors should be avoided when planning new libraries. They are unpopular with library users in general and they create severe problems for the disabled. In existing libraries, where there are split levels in the public areas, access to the various floors should, if possible, be by ramp rather than by steps. To provide a firm grip for the disabled and wheelchairs, interior ramps can be covered by grooved rubber tiles. Interior ramps should be sloped as gradually as possible although this can result in a loss of space.

Access to the upper floors of a multi-storey building can be by stairs, moving staircase or a lift. It will, naturally, be impossible for those in wheelchairs to negotiate the first two of these alternatives but some thought should be given to the design of staircases to make them more negotiable by the ambulant disabled. Goldsmith has provided the following data: staircases should be well-lit and fitted with handrails, and it is advisable to have heavy doors opening outwards at the head of the stairs. The stair riser should be the same height for each step, the surface of the step should be non-slip with as deep a tread as possible so that a person's weight will not rest on the edge of the step.[21] It will help those with sight defects if the treads and risers are delineated by different colour markings. A landing between the floor levels will be welcomed by those with cardiac and breathing disorders who find the effort of climbing stairs very tiring.

There are a number of stairclimbers available which will often carry both seated and standing passengers, and some will even negotiate bends in the stairs. Stair climbers can be operated so that a section of the staircase will be left for ordinary use. Few librarians, perhaps, will feel it necessary to install such equipment unless there are a substantial number of elderly and disabled people in the membership. The cost will not be inconsiderable and in most modern public library buildings there are more suitable alternatives. For the wheelchair user the lift will be the most satisfactory method of travelling between floors, for the ambulant disabled the lift or moving staircase will be sufficient.

The ordinary passenger lift will, in most cases, be suitable for use by the disabled. It should be clearly signposted indicating that it can be used by those in wheelchairs. If the lift is not operated by an attendant, the controls should be conveniently situated so that they can be reached by those in wheelchairs. When the only public access to the upper floors of the library is by moving staircase, then some alternative arrangements will need to be made for the wheelchair user and for the severely physically impaired. One possibility is to make the staff lift available. If necessary, the goods lift may, where feasible, be modified to enable wheelchair users and the ambulant disabled to use it.

A partial solution, in multi-storied buildings, is to ensure that the reading materials most in demand by the elderly and the disabled are located on the ground floor. Large print books for the visually handicapped are an example of the type of books which should be sited as near as possible to the library entrance. The lending services of the library which contain popular reading material should be on the ground floor as should other well-used services.

For the partially sighted reader attention should be given to the intensity and distribution of both natural and artificial light. This is an important consideration in the area allocated to the large print material. Some elderly people may be short sighted compelling them to be as close as possible to the titles of books in order to read them. Others may be long-sighted, requiring them to stand far away from the printed material they need to read. For the elderly with this complaint the gangways between the book bays will need to be as wide as possible to enable them to stand away from the shelves and read the titles of the books displayed.

It will be difficult for the partially sighted reader to use catalogues, particularly if small print is used for the entries. There are two possibilities: the entries should be printed in type large enough for the visually impaired to read or the staff should be trained to help readers who are obviously having difficulty. A notice encouraging the partially sighted to consult the staff is unlikely to encourage response, for the visually handicapped are often reluctant to draw attention to their disability.

REFERENCES

1 Great Britain, Office of Population Censuses and Surveys, Social Survey Division *Handicapped and impaired in Great Britain* Amelia Harries, Elizabeth Cox and Christopher R W Smith. London, HMSO, 1971, 25.

2 Ibid 25.

3 Ibid 27.

4 Ibid 27.

5 Ibid 4-5.

6 Ibid 5.

7 National Council of Social Service *The voluntary worker in the social services* (Aves Report) London, Allen and Unwin, 1969.

8 Critchley, W E 'Library services for the housebound reader in Scotland' *Book trolley* 2(3), September 1968, 55.

9 Ibid 56.

10 Ibid 56-7.

11 Wandsworth Libraries annual report 1967/68, 6.

12 Wandsworth Libraries annual report 1968/69, 4.

13 Kellner, Theda 'Media and the senior adult' *AHIL quarterly* 12 (2/3) spring/summer 1972, 17.

14 Goldsmith, Selwyn 'Library planning for the disabled' *Book trolley* 3(8), December 1972, 3-7.

15 Goldsmith, Selwyn *Designing for the disabled* 3rd ed London, RIBA Publications Ltd, 1976, 322(5803) (5804).

16 Ibid 168-172 (320).

17 Ibid 344 (63121).

18 Ibid 344 (63130) and 337 (6124).

19 Ibid 392 (74632).

20 Ibid 345 (6323) and 165-7(31).

SEVEN

LIBRARY SERVICES FOR THE BLIND

THE TERM 'visually handicapped' is generic and is applicable to anyone suffering from some form of sight defect. For the librarian, the provision of material for the visually handicapped must include:

i) meeting the needs of the blind who, in the majority of cases, will only be able to read embossed literature or listen to books recorded on to disc or cassette

ii) making special provision for those with some residual sight who can read books in larger print or with the assistance of a magnifying aid

The second aspect of this library provision will be considered in the next chapter as the evolution of library services to the partially sighted has been a much later development.

The difficulties which total blindness brings are so horrifying to the fully sighted that, inevitably, the blind have attracted considerable sympathy and the development of library services for them has a long history. But there have been several difficulties in the creation of effective services. The official definitions of blindness (those with a central visual acuity of less than 20/200) are not absolute for library purposes. Many of those who are classified as blind can read books with large print. Generally, however, the majority of those who are medically classified as blind will not be able to read conventional print at all.

As with other physically handicapped sections of society, the blind do not form a homogeneous group. Although blindness is often an affliction of old age it can strike at any age. Some blind persons will have been so since birth, others will have become blind in early or middle life. The onset of blindness can be a gradual process or may come suddenly, the result of an accident or illness. The age at which a person becomes blind will affect the nature of library provision appropriate for them. As will be discussed later, those who have been blind at an early age usually find it relatively simple to master the technique of braille. Those who become blind late in life are often unable to learn new and complicated skills, such as reading embossed literature.

Blindness can be accompanied by other sensory or physical disabilities. Children may be born deaf as well as blind, and those who become blind in old age may also be suffering from some associated and frequently crippling complaint; again this affects the provision of reading material. Children who are both blind and deaf have tremendous problems to surmount if they are to learn to read. The elderly blind person suffering from arthritis of the hands might well be incapable of reading a book in embossed type.

Perhaps more than any other physical disability, blindness has a profound effect upon the conduct of a person's life. There can be considerable psychological problems for those who have suddenly lost their sight; those who have been blind since birth may have experienced difficulties with their education. The range of occupations open to the blind is limited. Even in those categories of work where the blind can compete successfully with the fully sighted, employers may in some cases prefer to employ workers who are not suffering from impaired vision. The mobility of the blind will often be restricted and the complications of travelling in a large city can reduce their employment prospects. The task of changing buses or trains, which to the fully sighted is a relatively simple matter, can, for the blind, be an operation of major significance.

The development of library services to the blind has been influenced by these factors. It has also been dependent upon the blind being educated to a level which will enable

143

them to read. It was the introduction of educational provision for the blind in the eighteenth century that gave the necessary stimulus to the introduction of comparable library facilities in the following century.

The education of the blind

The first institutions of any kind to be established for the physically handicapped were for those who were blind. In the eighteenth century these were little more than asylums, but gradually vocational and eventually educational instruction was provided. Sometimes, blind schools would accommodate those with other physical disabilities, but progressively the blind were segregated into their own educational institutions.

Early foundations for the blind owed much for their existence to the efforts of voluntary bodies, and were indebted to the awareness of a few individuals who instigated services aimed at alleviating some of the problems of the visually handicapped. But the recognition that society as a whole had a duty to alleviate the difficulties which the blind faced was slow to come. In the United Kingdom, not until the Elementary (Blind and Deaf Children) Act of 1893 were authorities granted the power to provide for the education of blind children. This was later made a statutory requirement by the enactments of 1914 and 1918. The pattern of growth of educational provision was followed in other countries, with the state gradually assuming responsibility from the voluntary organisations which had made the initial provision.

In the United States the Bardon-La Follette Act of 1943 provided the starting point for programmes for the rehabilitation of the blind, and this was strengthened after the war by Public Law 565 (the Vocational Rehabilitation Act, 1954) and Public Law 333 (the Vocational Rehabilitation Amendments Act, 1965). These enactments were reinforced by further legislation introduced in the late 1960s. The effect of these federal laws in the United States was soon apparent: in

144

1943, prior to the introduction of the Bardon-La Follette Act, the number of blind persons who had completed rehabilitation courses was less than one thousand, in 1970 this had grown to around eight thousand. By this date, however, no distinction was being made between the blind and the partially sighted and many of the vocational programmes were for all those with severe sight impairment.

The impact of federal intervention in the provision of training facilities and vocational opportunities for the blind was far-reaching. The 1954 act, for example, had a direct influence upon library services for the blind. Fifteen million dollars were appropriated for research into the needs of the blind, some of which was directed to examining the possibilities of transcribing braille by computer and to the conversion of braille into tactile transmission (the Optacon).

Print for the blind

The educational and vocational programmes for the blind were to a great extent dependent upon the availability of a medium through which the blind could read. The development of such a system has a long and remarkable history. Unfortunately many of the experimental reading and writing systems for the blind, while showing distinct ingenuity, had little practical application.

The majority of methods which were devised to enable the blind to read, and possibly to write, concentrated upon the perfection of systems whereby they could read letters with their fingers. By the seventeenth century a form of writing which had some affinity with braille was introduced. Subsequent experiments designed to produce a system of embossed writing for the blind took two basic paths; there were those systems which sought to reproduce the alphabet in a form which could be 'read' by the blind with their fingers, whilst other methods converted the alphabet into shorthand. It was this last stream of development which was to prove the most significant.

145

The most successful form of 'short-hand' printing for the blind, perfected by Louis Braille, is the system which bears his name. Braille, who was himself blind, had been a pupil at l'Institution Nationale, where he had learnt the alphabet used by Valentin Haüy. Braille was one of the most gifted pupils at the institution and his worth was sufficiently recognised by his tutors for him to be offered a post as junior master.

As part of his work Braille became familiar with the various systems of embossed type in use at that time. There were clear defects in all the systems and Braille began to experiment with them, seeking for improvement. He finally decided that Charles Barbier's method involving a combination of two rows of six dots offered the greatest possibilities. Braille ultimately decided upon a system based upon a permutation of six dots, the symbols being arranged in two vertical columns of three dots. A history of France, published in 1837 is, conceivably, the first book to be published in braille. The six dots employed by Braille were remarkably flexible. They enabled all the letters of the alphabet to be represented as well as punctuation marks and some letter combinations.

There are now three versions of braille in use:
i) Grade I in which there are few contractions.
ii) Grade II which has a number of contractions used for groups of letters and grammatical forms. These are designed to reduce the bulk of the books produced in braille and also to make it possible to read the embossed letters more rapidly.
iii) Grade III braille, which is available in a few languages, is a highly contracted form and it has certain affinities with shorthand. Reading Grade III braille requires considerable skill and few blind people read in this form.

The flexibility of braille and its superiority over other forms of embossed type has led to its adoption throughout the world and it is now available in most languages. However, the acceptance of braille as the principle writing medium for the blind was not secured without a great deal of controversy.

Throughout the nineteenth century, the Battle of the Dots, as it came to be called, raged with remarkable acrimony. The situation was complicated by the existence of an equally vehement debate, later to be known as the Battle of the Contractions, over the differing standards and grades attainable.

Braille was introduced into the Near East, China and India towards the end of the nineteenth century, with Christian missionaries often being the pioneers, adopting the system to the requirements of the local language. With the near universal use of braille it has become increasingly necessary for uniformity to be achieved. In 1951 a step to reconcile the various forms of braille in use was made with the establishment of the World Braille Council. Since this date the council has done a great deal towards securing the acceptance of a standard world braille script.

It is now possible to produce books in braille using many of the techniques used for the mass printing of letterpress. Frank W Hall, who invented a braille writer in 1892, also devised a stereomachine which printed braille on to metal plates which could then be used to print books. Braille today can be produced on high speed rotary presses, the first press of this kind being used by the then National Institute for the Blind in 1930. The institute, now known as the Royal National Institute for the Blind, will soon be introducing braille which has been composed by computer, a process which will speed up transcription considerably.

The flexibility of braille has been a factor in its widespread use. But it is a system which can, unfortunately, only be used by a proportion of those who are blind. Those who become blind later in life find it difficult, if not impossible, to acquire the necessary technique to read braille. The elderly blind may have other problems, for example arthritis, which may make it painful or difficult. Older people, too, often lack the necessary sensitivity in their finger tips to identify braille letters.

Blind persons suffering from other physical disabilities may find it difficult to handle braille volumes. The page size of the average book in braille is 33 cm x 25.5 cm (13 inches by 10 inches), and even with this larger page size, comparatively few words can be accommodated. The paper which has to be used is considerably thicker than that used in normal letterpress book printing. This means that books produced in braille are often very bulky. The average novel, issued in hand or machine embossed braille, may require up to five large volumes; and the Old Testament transcribed takes fifty-seven volumes.

Books in embossed type are subject to heavy wear and tear. The majority of libraries providing a service to the blind reach their users by postal service, which introduces the possibility that books may be damaged in transit. Moreover, the embossed dots can be crushed with misuse: a person who has only recently learnt braille may press heavily upon the characters and flatten them. This can make them difficult for other readers to decipher.

The cost of braille production is high, even with the use of voluntary transcribers. As the books usually have to be sent to readers, the administrative expenses of a braille library will be greater than those of libraries serving sighted people.

For those blind persons unable to avail themselves of literature through the medium of braille, there are alternative forms of reading. The other line of development of embossed print, based upon the alphabetical form, has not produced a system comparable to braille. There is but one alphabetical form of embossed writing still in use, albeit to a limited degree, and this alphabetical system is named after the inventor, Dr William Moon. The Royal National Institute for the Blind is the only publisher of books transcribed in this system.

A very much more recent development is the use of computers for translating print into braille, which has now reached an advanced state of development. The development of computerised braille has depended upon braille contractions being reconciled with computer techniques and with the grammatical peculiarities of each language. This has been achieved for English, and computer-produced braille is now being successfully exploited in both the United Kingdom and the United States, with good progress being made in the Netherlands and Japan.

The Division for the Blind and Physically Handicapped (DBPH) of the Library of Congress is currently experimenting with a dual-purpose machine which converts print into synthesiser speech and also into braille. The project, with an adaptation of the Kurzweil Reading Machine, will give, it is hoped, the blind the same access as the sighted person to the collections of the Library of Congress. The project if successful should be operational 'within a year'.

The Royal National Institute for the Blind (RNIB) is the centre for computer braille in the UK. The method employed is to first transcribe the roman text into braille, this being corrected by retranslating the braille into a printout in roman face. The tape with the text in braille can be used to programme the automatic transcribing machine to produce a metal plate for embossing braille.

The merits of composing braille by computer are encouraging for the future. The space in which the tapes can be stored in case they are needed for further editions, is considerably less than the volumes in braille text. The process of computer braille is measurably faster than transcribing by hand or by braille writer.

The talking book

The possibilities for exploiting the commercial development of gramophone records, to produce 'talking books' for the blind, were examined as early as 1878 when Thomas Edison suggested that books could be recorded for the blind. There were basic difficulties of technical problems and the additional consideration of possible copyright infringements if books were sound recorded.

The technical obstacles to recording books were finally solved by 1935. The long-playing records which were introduced for placing books on discs were far in advance of those available on the commercial market. The records played at twenty-four revolutions per minute, the average novel requiring twelve discs.

The other major obstacle to the production of talking books was removed when a joint committee of the National Institute for the Blind and St Dunstan's reached an agreement with the Publishers' Association. This agreement ensured that the books so recorded would be available *only* for the blind.

In practice, few people in Britain were able to buy the necessary equipment to use the books on record. This meant, in the years before the Second World War, that the service of talking books reached only a minority of the blind. The advances which were made in the post-war years offered a number of possibilities for improving the quality of talking books. The first major innovation was to introduce books on disc which could be played at 33-1/3 rpm, which gave fifteen minutes' listening time for each side of the record. By 1960, thirty minutes' listening time could be obtained from each side of the record. Subsequent developments were to see the speed of the disc reduced to 16-2/3 rpm which gave forty-five minutes for one side of a ten-inch disc. Ultimately the speed of the disc was brought down to 8-1/3, and although it was technically feasible to have records operated at four rpm (the lowest speed at which the human voice could be recorded, giving a theoretical listening time of three hours for one side of a ten inch disc), this was not exploited as the assumption was that few people would have sufficient powers of concentration to listen for this length of time.

There were other problems inherent in the physical form of gramophone records:
i) Users experienced difficulty in finding the place at which they had previously finished listening. Attempts to locate a

particular section of the book frequently lead to the disc being scratched.

ii) Records inclined to warp if exposed to heat. This was a potential hazard, both during transit and while in the reader's home.

iii) Dust accumulating or liquid spilt on the record could seriously affect the clarity of speech.

These limitations made the development of the tape cassette a matter of urgent interest for libraries providing talking books to the blind. The possibilities of open reel tapes had never been actively explored in Britain, although they had been used to a limited extent by libraries for the blind on the continent. In 1959, the Nuffield Talking Book Library introduced a cassette weighing 6½ pounds, capable of giving twenty-one hours' listening time. The cassette proved to be superior to the record in a number of ways: it is less liable to damage in the post or in use, and offers greater flexibility for finding a particular place without damaging the tape.

Paradoxically, however, it was the length of listening time available on cassette which gave the greatest difficulties. The average novel requires nine hours' listening time, and, as the cassette would provide a much longer period of listening than this, it meant that more than one book would, in the interests of economy, be recorded on one tape. This led to difficulties in cataloguing. In addition, readers would often require only one of the books on the tape, while titles also recorded on the particular tape would be requested by other readers. It could result in books not being so readily available as when recorded on disc.

In spite of these drawbacks and some early technical mishaps, the Mark I system devised by the Nuffield Library (now the British Talking Book Service for the Blind) found an ever-increasing demand for books on tape. The number of patrons rising from 6600 in 1960 to 22,000 by 1967. The Mark IV cassette now used by the British Talking Book Service, is an eight-track (six for the text and two for the index) standard tape. Each track will give one hundred and thirty minutes of listening time and the tape is sufficiently small to be posted in a pillar box (saving the user a journey to the post office). The machine to play the talking book now weighs only eleven pounds and it is relatively simple to use. It has a high speed indexing system.

The rapid advances made in the efficiency and the availability of the talking book have focused attention upon the future of embossed literature. Talking books do not require the user to learn a new skill in order to use them, they are simple to operate and, given that the user's hearing is not impaired, provide a very effective medium for access to literature. In spite of this, there are certain benefits which the ability to read and write braille can bring. It can be used by blind students to take notes while reading, and does provide a direct means of communication between writer and reader. The speakers who record talking books may, consciously or unconsciously, introduce their own interpretation of the material. In the case of a novel or play they may invest the characters with a characterisation not intended by the author, and not desired by the listener.

The voice of the reader is, apparently, an important factor for the blind person using talking books. The blind develop a preference for, or a dislike of, certain narrators. Also, while certain types of material may gain from being read aloud (poetry and drama are examples) certain books, notably some modern novels, may contain passages which when spoken, cause more embarrassment than would be the case if the material were being read in letterpress or braille. There is, too, the sense of independence given by being able to read braille. The blind person is not dependent upon a machine in order to read. They can progress at their own speed, and it is easy to read difficult or especially arresting passages over, thus providing the opportunity to pause for thought or speculation.

Auditory reading is slower than reading embossed literature. Those skilled in using braille can achieve speeds of up to 120 words a minute. Although there have been attempts to produce a form of shorthand speech, these experiments, as yet, have not been wholly successful.

Despite the fact that embossed literature does have many advantages for the blind readers, the indications are that the majority of the blind are coming to prefer the talking book, at least for recreational reading. In 1937 the New York State Library circulated five thousand talking books, by 1958 this figure had reached 75,000, while, in the same period, the number of braille items lent by the library had fallen from 28,000 to seven thousand. It is reasonable to suppose that there will be a continuing demand for embossed literature. The benefits which have already been mentioned are relevant to the needs of the student and the serious reader.

It is perhaps wrong to consider the two systems as rival methods. Blind people can use both systems, and the talking book and embossed literature should really be regarded as being fundamentally complementary. The talking book is an admirable medium for recreational literature, although it is being used with notable success by students, particularly those who, for physical or psychological reasons cannot learn braille. Similarly, while braille does provide an excellent medium for recreational reading, it can be equally effective in giving the blind access to vocational or educational information.

Library provision

The evolution of library provision for the blind in different countries has not always followed the same path. The structure of existing library services, national policies towards the handicapped, the existence of voluntary organisations, have all influenced the pattern of service of libraries for the blind. In some countries the state has been willing to accept complete responsibility for supporting library provision for the blind. In others, the blind have had to rely almost entirely on voluntary efforts to create library facilities for them. Public libraries have, in certain parts of the world, been willing to assemble collections of embossed literature for the blind, and this may be part of a pattern of provision for the blind involving national, public and private libraries.

There are now two basic approaches: a fully centralised system, with a national collection of literature, or the decentralised pattern, with a network of regional libraries. The United Kingdom has adopted a centralised service, the United States has developed a partially decentralised system. Additionally, the library service for the blind in the UK is largely operated and financed by voluntary agencies. In the USA, federal, state and local governments all share the responsibility for ensuring that the blind, the partially sighted and the handicapped are receiving an adequate library service.

THE UNITED KINGDOM
The National Library for the Blind

There are a number of agencies which supply literature to the blind, the most important of which have accepted a national role. British public libraries at one time housed collections of embossed literature on a limited scale. The cost of maintaining these collections, coupled with the increasing efficiency of national services, led them gradually to relinquish this responsibility.

The National Library for the Blind (NLB) is the principal national repository of embossed literature in the United Kingdom. Its foundation was initiated, as with so many services for the disabled, by voluntary workers. The private house of the founder, Miss Martha Arnold, was the first headquarters of the first library for the blind in Britain. It began operations in 1882 with a collection of some fifty books in braille and moon. The emphasis of the collection was upon works with an evangelical or moral tone.

The main characteristics of this first library were a heavy reliance upon voluntary assistance both for transcribing and despatching the literature, and an equal dependence upon voluntary contributions for its financial support.

Unfortunately these related aspects of the provision of reading material for the blind are still very much in evidence today. Another important feature of the work of the library was that, from the outset, it was willing to supply literature to those living outside London. The 'country readers' were reached by the postal services or by a carrier. This early, distinctive characteristic is still apparent in the service which is being given to the blind in Britain.

The scale of operations of the library grew steadily, and by 1895 the number of volumes held by the library had reached 3200, and the service was reaching three hundred blind readers. In 1898 the library was registered at Somerset House as the Incorporated National Lending Library for the Blind. By this time the increasing volume of work was placing a considerable strain upon the voluntary staff, many of whom were elderly. Membership subscriptions had to be raised and the library, due to pressure upon the existing accommodation, had to move for the third time to new premises.

The library was fortunate in attracting dedicated men and women into its service. In Miss Ethel Winifred Austin, who became librarian and secretary in 1906, they found a woman who was able to combine her sense of dedication with a capacity for leadership. Miss Austin also had a vision of the way in which the library should develop. Fired by her zeal, the staff of the library were able to fashion it into the main centre for embossed literature in Britain. It absorbed a number of the other agencies which had proliferated in the nineteenth century. The braille collections assembled by such bodies as the Home Teaching Society, the Girls' Friendly Society and the Catholic Truth Society were all incorporated.

Miss Austin's plans to centralise all the collections of embossed literature under the auspices of her lending library were not immediately fulfilled. Nevertheless the library had by 1914 grown sufficiently in size and importance to justify an application to the Carnegie United Kingdom Trust for a grant to extend its services. In 1916 the library moved to new headquarters and changed its name to the National Library for the Blind. An announcement was made that it would no longer charge for its services, instead relying wholly upon voluntary donations for support.

The increased use of the library which followed the decision to make its service free necessitated a further expansion of its services. A northern branch was established at Manchester, again with the assistance of money from the Carnegie Trust. The site at Westminster was expanded, the costs of this being met partly by a grant of £15,000 from the trust, with an additional £3000 being contributed by the Ministry of Health. The rest of the capital needed was raised by public appeal and the use of trust funds.

A further addition to the library's income was provided by the requirements of the Blind Persons Act of 1920 which made county boroughs and county councils responsible for the welfare of blind people within their boundaries. The committee of the NLB was able to use the relevant clauses of the act as a means of persuading some local authorities to meet the costs of supplying books to the blind in their respective areas. Contributions from local and central government sources gradually became a more significant factor in the budget of the library.

By the outbreak of war in 1939, the library had developed to impressive proportions. The bookstock, including the northern branch, was 210,000 volumes and three thousand items were being transcribed annually by the copyists of the library. The NLB was circulating almost 340,000 books annually, not only in the UK but to forty-one other countries. During the war, both the London and the Manchester premises were damaged by bombs but in spite of this both centres continued to send books to their readers.

After the war an extensive programme of reorganisation was undertaken, this being principally accomplished under the direction of the new librarian and director general, W A Munford. The northern branch was extensively adapted and rebuilt and the services provided by the National Library for the Blind for their readers were extended and enlarged.

Reader services

A characteristic of many libraries for the blind is that they themselves have to produce a high proportion of the material they circulate. The NLB arranges for a number of books to be transcribed into braille each year with the assistance of its own panel of volunteers. In the year ending 1975, its transcribers and copyists added over three thousand volumes to the stock of the library.

The NLB also acquires machine-embossed braille, principally from publishers in the UK and the USA. The Royal National Institute for the Blind (RNIB) is the main supplier of machine-embossed braille to the NLB and the library acquires the books it circulates in moon from the same source. These latter books are acquired for those who cannot read braille and the NLB, by arrangement with the Canadian National Institute for the Blind, also supplies a small number of Canadians with books in moon.

Primarily a library of embossed literature, the NLB does stock, however, some large print books for the partially sighted.

Only a small proportion of the 30,000 books being published each year in the UK are transcribed into braille (approximately 0.04 per cent). In selecting books to be copied the known preferences of readers are taken into consideration, and the NLB concentrates upon providing for the recreational and cultural reading needs of its users. Students needing educational and technical material can obtain this from the Students' Library of the RNIB (see page 161). Otherwise the stock of the NLB covers the same range of subjects to be found in the average British public library. The selection of books is guided by the principle that the reading tastes of the blind do not differ substantially from the rest of the community.

Library services to the blind frequently have to rely upon the postal service to provide books to their readers. The blind are rarely able to visit their libraries and range over the bookstock in the same way as sighted readers. This requires that the blind have access to the necessary details of the bookstock of the library. To ensure this the NLB prints a wide range of catalogues and currently there exist:

i) a subject catalogue in five volumes covering the years 1965-1971

ii) a catalogue of books in moon

iii) a music catalogue.

In addition, in order to inform readers of additions to stock, the NLB issues twice monthly the *Braille Library bulletin*, which is published in both conventional type and in braille. This lists current publications which have been recently transcribed and also older works which are being made available in braille for the first time.

The NLB is no longer totally dependent upon donations and legacies, although these do form an important source of income. Grants from local authorities, libraries and other institutions account for approximately forty per cent of income. The library also receives financial assistance from voluntary organisations through Unified Collections, a fund which represents money collected by voluntary organisations for charitable purposes. This forms a substantial proportion of the library's financial support. Central government, through the Exchequer, makes occasional ad hoc grants, but it is still an independent body run by its own council, and is totally free from government control. Currently the NLB's expenditure is not matched by its income and it is now drawing upon its reserves in order to maintain its present level of service.

The library does not attempt to provide a talking book service. In 1935 the potentialities of the talking book were considered, but no action was taken. The responsibility for providing a supply of talking books has now been assumed by other agencies. This has made it difficult to establish a unified policy for the provision of reading material for the blind.

The Royal National Institute for the Blind

RNIB had its beginnings in 1868 when a group of blind people established the British and Foreign Society for

Improving the Embossed Literature of the Blind. The society was at first solely concerned with the publication of embossed literature, but as its activities widened, it was decided to rename the society the British and Foreign Association for Promoting the Education and Employment of the Blind. In 1914 the association became the National Institute for the Blind and it received its royal charter in 1953. Today the RNIB is a voluntary body, concerned with the well-being of the blind, and its activities reach virtually every aspect of blind welfare.

As a natural extension of its many programmes of blind education, the RNIB undertakes responsibility for the publication of books and other material. The publishing programme is consequently extensive, embracing the following activities:

i) the publication of books and magazines in braille and moon

ii) the provision, with the St Dunstans Organisation, of a full service of books on tape

iii) the supply of educational material to blind students in both braille and on tape

iv) the publication of sheet music in braille. The RNIB also maintains a collection of music in braille.

The branches of the RNIB which are engaged in meeting these responsibilities are the British Talking Book Service for the Blind, the Students' Braille Collection, and the Students' Tape Library.

The Talking Book Service for the Blind

In conjunction with St Dunstans, the RNIB maintains this service, using material which is recorded and produced in the library's own sound recording studios. The service of the library covers both the supply of books on tape and the provision of the necessary equipment to play the tapes. Recreational material is recorded by professional actors or broadcasters.

Any registered blind person, or anyone who can obtain a certificate confirming that they are suffering from severely defective vision, is eligible to use the facilities of this service. Permission to record books is granted by publishers on the assumption that the tapes and equipment will only be made available to those who are unable to read conventional print.

Users of the service are expected to pay a small annual subscription which includes the loan of the playback machine. In many cases this can be recovered from the person's local authority welfare service. The playback equipment is serviced by members of a nationwide panel of voluntary helpers, many of whom are experts in the fields of radio and electronics. These volunteers provide their services free of charge, and visit users in their homes to repair or overhaul the playback machine.

The range of material provided by the British Talking Book Service is not quite identical with that of the average public library. Certainly the material which is recorded will embrace those subjects which are popular with public library readers: fiction, biography and travel books, for example. However, many of the users are elderly, and have become blind late in life. In most cases they are unable to read braille, and are thus heavily dependent upon talking books. It has been suggested that the reading tastes of the elderly do not entirely mirror that of the rest of the adult community (see page 113). In consequence, the selection policies have to reflect this difference.

The RNIB has a committee to select material to be recorded or to be transcribed. An excellent account of the selection processes of the committee is provided by Donald E Schauder and Malcolm D Cram.[1] It is evident that the British Talking Book Service is predominantly concerned with providing a recreational service and this is designed especially to meet the particular needs of the elderly blind reader. The requirements of the more purposeful reader are met by the RNIB by providing specialist reading material in both braille and in talking book form.

Students' Braille Library

The requirements of the blind student are met through the collection of braille literature assembled to meet the requirements of the more serious reader. The students' library in braille consists of some fifty thousand items with over twenty thousand loans recorded each year to readers in both the United Kingdom and overseas. The users include university students, school pupils, those studying for a career and also those who are studying subjects for personal interest. The stock covers a wide range of topics and currently the library is strengthening its holdings in scientific subjects particularly in the fields of mathematics, physics and computer science.

The books are transcribed by volunteers who are often experts in their subjects. The volunteers give freely of their time and the library will arrange to have highly specialised works transcribed by request. The RNIB annual report for 1976 records the experience of one transcriber who spent 215 hours converting a particular work into braille. This, the report suggests, is by no means unique.

The manuscript department of the RNIB also provides a braille transcribing service. The department will arrange for exam papers to be copied and it will transcribe into braille instructions for the use of domestic appliances and equipment needed for educational purposes such as typewriters and recording equipment.

Students' Tape Library

The RNIB provides a library on cassette for the blind person pursuing academic or vocational courses. In 1976 there were 3529 books on tape held by the library and some five hundred titles are added each year, many of which have been added by request. The library does try to anticipate requests, and the books are recorded by volunteers, a high proportion being teachers and lecturers. Certain of the technical books recorded have braille diagrams added to them. Although the library is primarily intended for full-time students, it can be used by members of the Talking Book Service. The tape library for students is proving to be particularly valuable for those taking evening classes and for the blind who wish to continue interests acquired before they lost their sight.

Other sources of embossed literature
and talking books

There are a number of other publishers and agencies which produce embossed literature and books on tape for the blind. In some cases these agencies are not producing talking books solely for the blind and the tapes may be borrowed by those suffering from other physical disabilities.

The Scottish Braille Press:

This produces over forty magazines in braille in a number of languages and it publishes books, again in braille, on a variety of subjects. Its publishing programme includes weekly and monthly magazines. In addition it produces a number of journals for other organisations concerned with the welfare of the blind. As part of its book publishing activities, it issues novels, educational and religious works in braille. It is one of the largest publishers of braille in the world and it employs a high proportion of registered blind people in its printing works. It includes, also, a number of staff who are suffering from other physical handicaps.

British library of tape recordings:

Patients in London hospitals can benefit from a service of talking books provided by the British Library of Tape Recordings. This was established in 1963 with the aid of a grant from a hospital foundation. The actual supply of talking book tapes is free, but the hospitals taking part in the scheme are expected to buy the playback machines and they also pay an annual affiliation fee. The service is intended for all hospital patients who experience difficulty in reading or handling conventional print. It is therefore available to all handicapped people and not just the blind. The playback machine is an open tape player and it is equipped to enable the patient to listen to the tape without disturbing other patients in the ward.

National Listening Library:

Known as the National Library of Talking Books for the Blind, this was founded in 1972. Its collections are available to those who are handicapped to such a degree that they cannot hold or read printed books. It has been estimated that there are one hundred thousand handicapped people in the United Kingdom who would benefit from a talking book service. This includes those who are suffering from a wide range of crippling diseases. Currently the National Listening Library is reaching nearly one thousand people. It includes in its membership not only those who are physically disabled but also young people who lack the necessary reading skills to use the printed book.

The members of the library are expected to purchase their own playback machine, which is identical to that used by the RNIB. There is an annual subscription for the service. The tapes include a variety of subjects and some are copies of those produced by the RNIB. Members can choose up to ten titles from the catalogue supplied to them. Two titles at a time are posted to users, and these are replaced by two further titles when the tapes are returned.

CALIBRE:

CALIBRE is a service to the handicapped which came into being in 1975, and lends out tapes which can be played on commercial cassette players. It is intended for those whose detective vision prevents them from reading print and also those who are so physically handicapped that they have difficulty in holding books. The only qualification for membership is that prospective users need to supply a doctor's certificate certifying that they are unable to read printed material.

It is a postal service, with members meeting the costs of postage; except that those who are blind are entitled to receive the service post free. There is no charge levied for the loan of the tapes but CALIBRE indicates that it will be grateful if members can contribute to the costs of producing the cassettes. Hospitals and other institutions have to pay a group membership subscription. Individual members are allowed two and group members four cassettes at a time. The service was intended at first for children and teenagers but it has now extended its facilities to adults.

Conclusion

The development of library services for the blind in the United Kingdom has been dependent almost entirely upon the efforts of individuals and voluntary bodies. Without the dedication and hard work of those who recognised the plight of the blind the facilities available today for the visually handicapped would not be as extensive as they are. It would be wrong to minimise the achievements of voluntary societies and private individuals, or the financial contribution made by the general public; but nevertheless it is apparent that library services to the blind in Britain have suffered from a chronic shortage of resources. The contribution made by government, while increasingly important in some sectors, has not compensated for the need for adequate support for the development of comprehensive library services for the blind. The contrast between the attitude of the British central government and that taken by the US federal government is particularly marked. In the US the federal government, through the agency of its own library, the Library of Congress, has been willing to acknowledge the responsibility it has to meet the reading needs not only of the blind but all those who are severely handicapped.

THE UNITED STATES OF AMERICA
Introduction

The evolution of library services for the blind in the USA differs in certain fundamental respects from the pattern established in the UK. All levels of government—federal, state and local—are concerned with the provision of reading material for the blind. In addition a high proportion of the necessary financial expenditure is being met from public funds. The library service is largely decentralised, although the Library of Congress through its Division for the Blind and Physically Handicapped, acts as a coordinating agency. It does this through its system of regional libraries, with a number of state, urban public libraries and private institutions established as regional focal points for the provision of reading material to the blind and physically handicapped. A final distinction is that the Library of Congress has not, for some time, differentiated between the reading needs of the blind and other persons who are physically handicapped.

This system of provision has ensured that the blind in the USA have access to the best library service for the visually handicapped in the world. However, the acceptance by the federal government of its duty to make reading material available in embossed and later tape form was not immediate. A short account of the developments which led to the formation of existing services will show the changing philosophies which made them possible.

Historical development

The public libraries were the first agencies to recognise and make special provision for the reading needs of the blind. Boston Public Library, in 1868, was the pioneer in establishing a collection of embossed literature, the catalyst for this provision being an inaugural gift of eight volumes in raised script.

Other libraries began to follow Boston's example, but the most important development was not these isolated ventures. The opening, in 1897, of a 'Pavilion for the Blind' by the Library of Congress was to prove a more significant event. This was at first intended to be no more than an experiment, but the use of the pavilion by the blind grew rapidly. There was much to attract them: the room was generously equipped with embossed books, maps, charts, magazines and newspapers. In addition, each afternoon, reading sessions were held. Between November 1897 and September 1898, the pavilion was able to attract nearly five hundred blind visitors.

This was, apparently, sufficient to encourage a continuation of the experiment. Musicales were added to the range of activities, and by 1902 the readings alone had been attended by nearly ten thousand blind people, while the total attendance had reached 26,000.

The collection of embossed literature, was in the early years, heavily dependent upon gifts to augment its stock. In 1903, of the fifty-seven volumes added, only four had actually been purchased. In spite of this, the collection grew steadily and by 1908 there were almost three thousand items available for the blind reader, including books, periodicals, music and maps. In its annual report of 1910 the Library of Congress defined the purpose of this collection. It included supplying books and periodicals in raised characters for reference and for home use within the District of Columbia, and the supply of information for projects designed to alleviate the condition of the blind. There would also be provision for lectures, readings and musicales for the instruction and entertainment of the blind in the state.

It seems that the success of the pavilion was providing an embarrassment. The report concluded that the service being provided by the Library of Congress was principally used by the blind residents of the District of Columbia: 'It is a service not to research or scholarship, but to the general reader . . . it is therefore a service logically rather within the province of the public library of the District [of Columbia]'.[2] It was therefore proposed that the books in raised type should be deposited with the public library.

The embossed books were duly transferred to the public library, but the blind of the District soon voiced their dissatisfaction. It is recorded in the annual report for 1912 that a 'keen desire' had been expressed by the blind for a 're-association' with their former meeting place. Eventually the embossed books were recalled from the District of Columbia Public Library and the Library of Congress resumed its services to the blind.[3]

The collection of embossed literature, while still used predominantly by those living in the District of Columbia, was increasingly being made available to the blind who were resident in other parts of the United States. This was particularly true of those in the states of the middle west and the south where few loan collections of embossed books existed. It was estimated in this period that there were 15,000 readers of embossed type in the USA, of whom the Reading Room for the Blind of the Library of Congress was supplying four per cent with reading material.

By 1917 the number of embossed books held by the Library of Congress had risen to 4300. Of the 450 books added that year, 287 had been purchased.[4] This demonstrates that the library was increasingly placing less reliance upon donations to maintain its stock of embossed literature.

The First World War brought a sharp increase in demand. Volunteers were recruited by the library to be trained in the transcription of reading material into braille. This work was undertaken in conjunction with the Red Cross Institute for the Blind. The books transcribed by the volunteers were also available to other patrons of the library, thereby enhancing the quality of the service to the blind population as a whole. The American Library Association participated in the programme to transcribe books into braille for those blinded during the war. By the efforts of the ALA fifty-six books were transcribed into braille.

By these and other means the collection of embossed literature held by the reading room which, from 1925 was called the Library for the Blind grew rapidly in size. Since 1913 the library, aided by an annual appropriation from the federal government, had been acquiring all those books transcribed under government contract by the American Printing House for the Blind at Louisville, Kentucky.

Miss Gertrude ·T Rider had been appointed librarian to the reading room in 1912, a post which she held until her retirement in 1925. Under her dynamic leadership the library services to the blind were dramatically reorganised.[5] With the changes in book selection policy already mentioned the bookstock rose to over 13,000 items and the number of volumes lent to the blind in all parts of the USA in 1924/25 reached 42,000.[6]

The Library of Congress was now actively considering the possibilities of coordinating its services to the blind with those provided by other libraries holding substantial collections of embossed literature. The intention was that some of the demands being made upon the Library for the Blind could be relieved, by decentralising the organisation of library services. Considerable impetus to these proposals was provided by two pieces of related legislation: the Pratt Bill which was introduced in the House of Representatives (HR 11365) and the Smoot Bill which was simultaneously presented to the Senate (S 4030). The Pratt-Smoot Bill became law on March 3 1931. It authorised the Library of Congress to cooperate with other libraries willing to serve as local or regional centres for the provision of reading material for the blind. A sum of $100,000 was appropriated to expedite this programme.

The implications of the Pratt-Smoot Bill were that the federal government was to assume responsibilities for the provision of reading material to the blind of the United States. The only limitation was that the service would be, for the immediate future, confined to adults. It was not until the word 'adult' was deleted from the enabling legislation in 1952 that the Library of Congress was able to give a service to blind children.

The regional libraries which were chosen to act as centres for services to the blind were predominantly state libraries and large urban public libraries. At first the money appropriated was devoted to the purchase of embossed literature, principally in braille. In the early 1930s the Library of Congress was also actively considering the potentialities of the talking book. The American Foundation for the Blind had developed two machines capable of recording a book of sixty thousand words on to eight or nine double-faced, twelve inch records. By 1943 the talking books were sufficiently advanced to merit Congress setting aside funds for the purchase of books on records. The user of the talking book being responsible for acquiring the necessary playing equipment. In practice, the cost of the playing machine was often met by public authorities and private foundations.

The changing role of the library for the blind was defined by the Library of Congress annual report for 1939:

i) To maintain a representative collection of embossed and talking books

ii) To reproduce books in braille in cooperation with the American Red Cross through the work of voluntary transcribers

iii) To provide an information service on all matters pertaining to the welfare of the blind.[7]

Since the end of the Second World War, the services to the blind provided by the Library of Congress have been extended. Blind children are now entitled to receive a supply of material. In addition the physically handicapped who find it difficult to use the conventionally printed book can use the facilities of the Division for the Blind and Physically Handicapped and its regional libraries. This latter change was made in 1966 when the reading needs of the handicapped were added to the responsibilites of the Library of Congress.

In response to the extra demands made upon its services the DBPH has strengthened its collections to include large print books for the partially sighted reader. It also began an appraisal of the role of the regional libraries to assess the possibilities of enlarging the scope and the number of area collections for the blind and physically handicapped. This review was given added assistance by the decision of the federal government to introduce the Library Services and Construction Bill in 1966 (title IVB of Public Law 89-911) which made available the necessary financial support for public libraries to add books in braille, talking books and large print material to their collections.

The regional libraries

The Pratt-Smoot Act of 1931 empowered the Library of Congress to cooperate with other libraries for the development of reading facilities for the blind. The intention was that the independent agencies providing embossed literature, many of which had proliferated in the nineteenth century, should pool their resources and efforts. The Library of Congress would act as the coordinating centre for a network of libraries for the blind.

The campaign proved remarkably successful and a system of eighteen regional libraries was established in various parts of the United States. There was a complete lack of criteria for determining the ability of any library to give an adequate supply of reading material to the blind. The Library of Congress therefore enlisted the assistance of the American Library Association and the American Foundation for the Blind in making this initial selection.

There have been problems in determining the precise responsibilities of the regional libraries for the blind. The geographical areas to be covered were not clearly defined, and a number of them found that they were receiving requests from the blind living in other states. The libraries which found themselves in this position did not always receive adequate recompense for supplying material to those living outside their official boundaries. This developed into a long-standing problem; writing as late as 1956, Florence Grannis drew attention to the position of Seattle Public Library whose Division for the Blind was providing library services to the blind of Montana, Washington and Alaska. [8] This was apparently not an uncommon experience for the city libraries which were acting as regional centres. Charles H Ness, in the same period, reported that the Free Library of Philadelphia was satisfying requests for embossed and talking books from all parts of the USA. It was even receiving enquiries for reading material from as far away as Canada. [9]

To resolve this problem, the DBPH has been steadily entering into contracts with other libraries, and the system of regional libraries has also been reorganised. In 1974, two multi-state centres for the blind and physically handicapped were established. The Florida Regional Library was to serve the states in the south; Utah Regional Library was to meet the inter-state needs of the blind and physically handicapped in the west. Two other centres have now been selected: Volunteer Services for the Blind in Philadelphia will act as the multi-state centre for the north, with the Starved Rock Library System in Illinois serving the midlands.

To meet local reading needs a system of sub-regional libraries has been built up. Many of the sub-regional centres are public libraries, which emphasises the increasing recognition being given to American public libraries as agents for the provision of the specialised reading material needed by the blind. The sub-regional libraries maintain collections of books on tape. They also act as intermediaries between the blind and the regional libraries. Many other public libraries maintain demonstration collections of talking books and playback equipment. The public library is obviously seen as an important source of information on the library facilities which are available to the blind.

Reader services

The federal government has established that it has a responsibility not only for the reading needs of the blind, but also to all those who are prevented by physical disability from reading literature published in conventional form. The Division for the Blind and Physically Handicapped of Congress' own library has been selected as the natural agency to fulfil these obligations. For the fiscal year 1976, Congress voted over seven million dollars for the provision of the following collections:

i) Books in embossed type and recorded form (on disc or tape)
ii) Periodicals in embossed and recorded form
iii) Musical scores suitable for use by blind musicians
iv) Embossed maps
v) A reference collection of printed material on all aspects of blindness and physical handicap.

The DBPH acquires embossed literature and talking books from a number of publishing concerns in the United States, and there are certain presses which transcribe material in embossed type under contract. There is also an active programme for acquiring material published for the blind in other countries. For example, it collects the works published by the RNIB.

The two most important publishers of talking books in the US are the American Federation for the Blind and the American Printing House. The DBPH places regular orders with these organisations and also with the Recordings for the Blind Inc (New York) which, with the assistance of a number of volunteers, records and makes available textbooks and other educational works.

The DBPH, like the NLB in the United Kingdom, produces much of the material which it circulates. This work is again undertaken primarily by volunteers who are trained locally, either by instructor or by correspondence course. The DBPH issues certificates of efficiency to transcribers both as a means of encouragement and as a method of maintaining and raising standards.

There also exists a programme for the production of material which is not of general appeal. This material is produced in braille and in recorded form. There are some two thousand titles recorded by volunteers on open-reel masters. Until recently these have only been available to libraries through the multistate centers, but the intention is to select some six hundred of these titles for recording in cassette form to make them more widely available.

The DBPH has a number of exchange agreements with organisations in other countries for the acquisition of material in foreign languages which have been transcribed or recorded for the blind.

The DBPH frequently publishes catalogues of its holdings, and as part of the Library of Congress programme for computerising the records of books and other material, the division has embarked upon a project for the provision of a computerised bibliographical service for the blind and physically disabled. It is working in close cooperation with the

Library Systems Applications Group of the Library of Congress to develop and publish a union catalogue of material in braille, in cassette form or on disc. The first copies of the catalogue have been produced on microfiche as computer output microfiche (COM) and these have been distributed to the 154 regional and sub-regional libraries of the DBPH network. The title of the microfiche catalogue is *Reading materials for the blind and physically handicapped*, and each edition is a complete cumulation.

Again in cooperation with the Library Systems Applications Group, the DBPH has been developing a 'copy allotment system'. This enables the DBPH to supply the regional libraries with bibliographical data on new titles, permitting them to make a choice of the titles and the number of copies they require. The information on these selections is processed through the copy allotment system to give production and distribution information.

In order to inform members of the availability of recently published titles for the blind, the DBPH publishes a number of information bulletins. The two main sources for material recently added to stock are the *Talking book topics* and *Braille book review*. These are made available in both large print and braille, while the former is also published in flexible disc. These are cumulated into annual catalogues which again are published in large print, in braille and on tape. The entries in the catalogues are often annotated and the style and format is designed to meet the needs of the general reader. The regional libraries also publish their own catalogues of material available for the blind and the physically handicapped.

DBPH also publishes bibliographies of material available for the blind in specific subject fields. For example *Freedom '76* is a bicentennial publication containing selected items in braille and in recorded form on the revolutionary period. Included with the thirty-six page bibliography, which is in large print, is an eight rpm soundsheet for playback equipment.

In selecting material for addition to its stock, the division makes the basic assumption that the visually and physically disabled will have the same reading interests as the rest of the population. The high average age of the users of the DBPH influences the general approach to the selection of items for transcription into braille or recording on disc or tape. The consequence is that the scope of the collections of the DBPH and its regional libraries is generally broader than that of the average US public library. No attempt is made to censor material, but certain books may be subject to restrictions which would not be relevant to the production of books for sighted readers. Cost is a factor which is carefully considered, as books in braille and on tape are more expensive to produce than books in conventional print. The cost incurred in producing a specialist work will be related to the potential use made of the work once it is transcribed or recorded.

There are also technical problems which make it difficult to reproduce a work in a satisfactory form for the blind. A book containing complex diagrams, drawings, charts, possibly photographs will obviously present difficulties. If this data is an essential part of the work a decision may be taken not to reproduce it.

The law of copyright may occasion difficulties. In the United States the DBPH, the American Printing House for the Blind, and Recordings for the Blind have reached an agreement with some publishers who have granted 'blanket' permission on all their works. In other countries it may be necessary to apply for the right to transcribe or record each book as it is published. There can also be restrictions on the use of such copies.

In 1974 book selection policy was reviewed when representatives of the blind met at the Library of Congress. The study group drew up a general book selection statement to provide guidelines for the acquisition of material. A more detailed guide has been drawn up for staff concerned with selecting titles to be transcribed into braille or to be recorded.

174

Music:

The Library of Congress introduced a music collection in braille for the use of blind students and musicians in 1962 as a result of the provision contained in Public Law 87-765. As with the other services, these are available also to the physically handicapped. To further assist the blind a braille edition of *Music article guide* is produced. This is a quarterly publication, which indexes and annotates articles appearing in the leading American magazines on music. The blind and physically handicapped can request sound recordings of the articles that interest them.

The DBPH is currently serving over 1500 blind musicians, students of music and music lovers. The collection consists of braille music and there are more than 24,000 classical and popular items. The music is obtained from the braille presses of the US and the UK. There are a number of 'unique multi-format packages' which consist of a combination of print, braille and recorded music. Each package is intended to meet the requirements of the blind or partially sighted student or teacher.

There is also a collection of music on open reel tape, cassette and disc. The sound collection can meet the needs of the students at any stage in their development. There are specialised music tapes for the advanced student. For those beginning their music studies there are self-instruction on tape courses covering a variety of instruments.

The large print music collection for the partially sighted musician concentrates upon techniques and simple pieces of music. The intention is to build up this large print collection by adding material for the more advanced student.

There is a music magazine *Musical mainstream* published twice a month, and this is issued in braille, large print and in recorded form. This includes both articles which have appeared in other magazines and also original features. Recent acquisition of musical items by the DBPH are listed.

Periodicals:

The magazine publishing programme of the DBPH embraces sixty-seven periodicals. The policy of the division has

175

changed from publishing magazines covering topics of concern to the visually and physically handicapped to offering periodicals of more general interest. The flexible disc format which is now being used permits the issue of periodicals rapidly and at a relatively low cost. The division is currently reviewing its magazine publishing policy. A consultant is currently liaising with twelve focus panels which represent readers in various parts of the USA.

Other publications:

In order to publicise its services the DBPH has an extensive advertising publishing programme. A number of brochures are produced outlining the extent of the division's resources and the special collections which it contains. Examples of these publicity leaflets are 'Talking books and muscular dystrophy', 'Talking books and cerebral palsy', 'Talking books and multiple sclerosis'.

Services to children:

Since 1952 the DBPH has been providing a service to visually and physically handicapped children. There is a specialist staff to deal with childrens' affairs. The material to be transcribed or recorded is reviewed by the Library of Congress Advisory Committee on Selection of Children's Books for the Blind and Physically Handicapped. The division also provides a service of recorded material to those children with learning problems. A disc at slow reading speed (100 to 125 words a minute) is available with a picture book related to the text. This is for those children with reading or speech problems.

Volunteers:

The division draws extensively upon the assistance of voluntary workers. Volunteers, often with specialist knowledge in particular subjects, handcopy braille titles. In 1975/76, 3699 volumes were transcribed by volunteers. The DBPH also has a programme for the production of tapes by volunteers: in 1975/76 133 books and six magazines were recorded.

Current research and programme evaluation:

DBPH conducts a continuous review of the methods and the equipment available for the visually and physically handicapped. Contracts are frequently awarded by the division to research and commercial undertakings to produce new machines and equipment. The DBPH also pursues its own evaluation programmes.

The division is concerned that of an estimated seven million people who are eligible to use its services only half a million are actually in membership. The American Foundation for the Blind, Inc (AFB) has been awarded a contract to determine who of those eligible to use the service would do so if they were aware of the materials available. The survey will also investigate reading interests and preferences.

The AFB has worked for many years with the blind. It has assembled a team of experts familiar with the problems of the handicapped groups which are sought as members of the library network.

There is close cooperation with other bodies, both official organisations and voluntary institutions, engaged in work with the visually and physically handicapped. There are a number of other important distributors of reading material for the blind in the United States. Several of these are specialist publishing houses which produce literature in specific subject areas for specific needs. Examples of specialist publishers for the blind are the Jewish Braille Institute of America and the Xavier Society for the Blind.

The American Printing House for the Blind

Founded in 1858, the American Printing House for the Blind (of Louisville, Kentucky) was the earliest national organisation to be established for the blind in the United States. It is now the only completely independent institution which publishes literature for the blind, although it does receive financial assistance from the federal government for many of its programmes. Fiscal aid from the US government began as early as 1879 with the introduction of

177

legislation 'to promote the education of the blind'. This assistance came in the form of a grant of $10,000. Prior to this the institution had been commissioned by the state of Kentucky to publish embossed literature for schools and other organisations.

The company now produces reading material in braille, large print and recorded form. With the help of annual appropriations from the federal government the institution publishes books and other educational material for blind children and young adults who are being educated in public schools.

Its work is directed by three policy-making and administrative committees, one of which is the Publications Committee. It has a number of departments: editorial, data processing, recording, educational research, fund raising, magazine and the Instructional Materials Center.

As part of its information services, the American Printing House for the Blind publishes lists of diagnostic reading tests and a reference catalogue of braille textbooks, produced by volunteers. It sponsors conferences for educationalists and voluntary workers concerned with the welfare of the blind. It also issues catalogues of large print material, educational cassette tapes, braille music, and educational aids.

Much of the educational information services of the printing house are transmitted through its Instructional Materials Reference Center. As part of its work the center maintains the 'Central catalogue of volunteer produced textbooks'. This contains over eighty thousand titles of material in braille, large print and recorded format. The catalogue is available in book form to institutions such as the regional libraries for the blind.

Public libraries

A number of public libraries form an integral part of the DBPH network, acting as regional or sub-regional libraries. In addition, there is an increasing involvement of the public library service as a whole in the supply of reading material to

178

the blind. The following facilities have been developed by public libraries in recent years:

i) A browsing collection of popular books in braille and on tape and some essential reference books

ii) An information service on the reading material available through the DBPH and its network of libraries. A member of the staff of the public library may also have made themselves completely familiar with the special reading needs of the blind reader.

iii) The provision of a playback machine for talking books for demonstration purposes.

iv) The publication of a talking newspaper for the blind.

v) The introduction of radio reading services with up-to-date information for the blind gathered from newspapers, magazines and recent books.

REFERENCES

1 Schauder, Donald E and Cram, Malcolm D *Libraries for the blind—an international study of policies and practice* Stevenage, Peter Perigrinus Ltd, 1977, 30-32.

2 Library of Congress *Report of the Librarian of Congress and report of the superintendent of the library building and grounds for the fiscal year ending June 30 1910* Washington, Government Printing Office, 1910, 73.

3 Ibid 1912, 107-108.

4 Ibid 1917, 117.

5 Library of Congress *Report of the Librarian of Congress for the fiscal year ending June 30 1925* Washington, Government Printing Office, 1925, 12.

6 Ibid 149-150.

7 Ibid 1939, 376.

8 Grannis, Florence 'Statewide financial support for Seattle's regional library for the blind' *Wilson Library bulletin* 30(9), May 1956, 700-701.

9 Ness, Charles H 'New resources for blind readers' *Library journal* 84(17), October 1959, 2882.

EIGHT

LIBRARY SERVICES
FOR THE PARTIALLY SIGHTED

IT IS APPARENT from the previous chapters that official and private sympathy with the plight of the blind has been an important factor in the development of reading services for this section of the community. This concern has not been paralleled to any noticeable degree, until recent years, by an awareness of the reading needs of the severely visually handicapped who yet retain some residual sight.

The reasons for this apparent lack of interest in the problems of the partially sighted are complex. There was a strongly-held view in the medical profession that residual sight should be 'preserved'. Reading would weaken the sight of those with severely defective vision. While the condition of complete blindness invariably attracts sympathy, poor eyesight does not. Indeed, those suffering from inadequate vision may be the object of ridicule.

The variety of conditions which cause defective eyesight are numerous. Equally the severity of the effect of different eye complaints vary markedly between individuals. Some complaints, for example myopia, can be corrected with the aid of spectacles, and some people with defective vision will be able to read with the assistance of magnifying aids. Children can overcome some of the reading problems of myopia simply by holding books closer to their eyes.

The definitions of blindness were confusing for those attempting to determine the need for a special library service for those with defective vision. A popular misconception is that the blind are completely without sight. In practice, many people officially defined as blind do often retain some residual vision. An exploratory study involving sixty-five adults living in London who had recently lost their sight revealed that only 1.5 per cent of those interviewed were completely blind. Over half could count fingers held before them at a distance of three feet. Slightly more than thirty per cent could see fingers held between three and ten feet from them.[1]

Normal vision is defined as 20/20 which means that a letter twenty feet high can be seen at a distance of twenty feet. Normal side vision would imply an ability to see objects between forty-five and eighty-five degrees on either side without moving the head. Those considered to be suffering from partially sighted vision, in medical terms, are those who fall within the category 20/70–20/100. This means that the individual can only identify letters at twenty feet which are discernible by the fully sighted person at seventy to one hundred feet. Blindness is normally defined as 20/200 and it also includes those whose visual field is twenty degrees or less.

These assessments are reached by tests conducted under artificial conditions and they do not reveal 'functional vision'. Paradoxically, many people who have been medically classified as blind can read print adequately, while others categorised as partially sighted will be unable to read, even with correctional lenses or magnifying aids. Unfortunately, in some countries, unless those with severe sight defects can produce medically supported evidence that they are unable to read conventional print under any circumstances, they will be refused access to collections for the blind. This means that they will be effectively denied the use of embossed literature and talking books. If they are to read at all they will need either the provision of books in large type or magnifying aids.

The development of effective methods for enabling the partially sighted to read has centred largely upon these two possibilities. There have been economic difficulties to surmount. The number of partially sighted in the community is comparatively small. The introduction of programmes for the production of large print books and the making of an effective aid for the magnification of print requires considerable capital expenditure, and this has deterred publishers and manufacturers from venturing into these uncertain realms. In spite of this, the last decade has seen the emergence of viable publishing programmes for large print material, and some progress has been made towards the introduction of an effective reading aid for the partially sighted. There has, too, been a greater willingness to make facilities formerly reserved for the blind available to all those with visual or physical handicaps.

The large print book

There has for some time been a recognition of the value to the partially sighted of books printed in larger type face. Students with defective vision could, sometimes, have essential textbooks copied for them on typewriters with larger characters. It was also possible to have reading material photographically enlarged by printing firms specialising in xerography. Clearly, these were both costly undertakings, and for the general reader unable to read print of normal size, there were few possibilities. Some religious and devotional works were published in larger print, making them easier to read aloud to a congregation. The British and Foreign Bible Society published several editions of the Old and New Testaments in an enlarged type face. Some publishers, notably Macmillan and Heinemann, issued certain of their famous authors in large print editions.

Immediately after the Second World War, an awareness grew of the difficulties which the partially sighted encountered. A bibliography for the partially sighted, 'Easy on the eyes', was published in the Wisconsin Library *Bulletin* in 1946. A similar pamphlet *Save your eyes* by M Hill and D Croucher was issued by the Oregon Education Department. The American Library Association introduced a fourth edition of its list of large print books *Books for tired eyes* in 1951. A few non-profit making organisations, including the Printing House for the Blind and the National Aid to the Visually Handicapped (San Francisco), published in large print those classics which were regularly included in the curricula of schools and colleges. In the UK, Hornsey Public Library produced *Books for short-sighted readers*, a list based upon material in its own stock, containing over 250 titles specifying editions which had been published in large print.

It was, of course, always an option for the determined individual to use a magnifying aid. Usually this would take the form of a simple hand lens to help read books in conventional sized print. There are serious disadvantages to reading print in this way and these would be sufficient to discourage the majority of those with defective vision (see pages 193-5).

By the early 1960s, interest had been awakened to the possibilities of printing large type books in sufficient numbers to meet at least some of the requirements of the partially sighted. Naturally, as with other physical disabilities, different individuals had different problems. Some of the eye conditions which occasion severely defective sight are associated with old age, and a growth in the proportion of elderly in the population of many countries brought a natural increase in the number of partially sighted. Many of the congenital diseases of the eye which affect young children have either been eradicated or are now responsive to treatment. The placing of prematurely-born children in oxygen tents has now been abandoned as it can cause retrolental fibroplasia, a severe eye complaint, but there are still a number of young people suffering from this form of defective vision.

There has been a significant change in medical opinion in recent years. Those with impaired vision are now encouraged to use such sight as they possess. Reading is accepted as a suitable activity, and children with defective vision are positively encouraged to read, if necessary holding the printed material close to their eyes. Concurrently, there have been advances in printing technology, particularly in the development of photolithographic and electrostatic techniques. This has made possible the publication of books in enlarged print at a much lower cost. Related to this has been the research which has been conducted into methods for making special editions for the partially sighted more effective. The optimum size of type for large print books, the significance of the opacity and texture of paper, the relationship between colour of ink used and the colour of the paper have all been investigated. The ultimate effect of these changes in attitude and the advances in technology has been to encourage more commercial publishers to venture into the field of large print production. In some cases the results of these experiments have not been sufficiently encouraging for the programme to continue, but there is now a steady output of large print editions, which go some way to providing the partially sighted with a choice of reading material.

In the UK the first recognition of the need for properly documented research into the needs of the visually handicapped came with the formation of the Books for Readers with Defective Sight Sub-committee of the Library Association in 1960. The committee examined several possibilities for helping the partially sighted, including the necessity for a list of existing books in print large enough to be read by those with defective vision. The prime concern was to establish a viable publication programme of books designed specifically for the visually handicapped. It was eventually agreed that an exploratory scheme for the xerographic reproduction in enlarged type of a representative selection of books would indicate the feasibility of such a project. In order to implement this project, the Library Association was awarded a grant of £10,000 in 1964 by the Viscount Nuffield Auxiliary Fund. This money was intended to launch a limited programme of large print publication.

By this time, F A Thorpe was already beginning to issue a series of large print works from his Leicestershire headquarters at Ulverscroft. It was apparent to the LA that the

Ulverscroft series was, in effect, fulfilling their own proposed publishing venture. It was decided not to proceed with this, but, instead, to use the grant from the Nuffield Fund to support Thorpe's work. This would be done by publicising Ulverscroft titles as they appeared. Public reaction would be monitored and the results of this continuous reviewing process would be passed on.

The production of large print titles specifically for the visually handicapped in the USA followed a similar pattern to developments in the UK. In 1965 Keith Jennison of Franklin Watts instigated a programme of large print publishing known as the 'Keith Jennison Editions in Large Type'. It was intended that this series should consist of titles of general interest, printed in eighteen point type, with a first issue of some four hundred titles, including those literary works most frequently required as reading in schools and colleges. Response to the series was sufficiently encouraging to persuade other American publishers to announce plans for issuing their own large print books. Harper and Row, Macmillan, and later Walker and Company all introduced limited programmes for the production of reading material for the partially sighted. In 1966 Ulverscroft Books, through a US agent, began marketing operations in America. The series concentrated predominantly upon popular titles, including romantic novels, mysteries and westerns. Some non-fiction works were issued under the Ulverscroft imprint, the subjects usually those with a wide appeal.

To complement the Ulverscroft series, the National Library for the Blind has since 1966 made the 'Austin' books available. This series, named after the founder of the NLB, is produced by photolithography with the assistance of University Microfilms. The Austin books are not available for purchase by the general public, but they can be borrowed from the NLB through the agency of public libraries. There are, currently, some three hundred titles available in this series. The titles include classic novels, literature, with a range of popular non-fiction covering such subjects as history, travel, biography, philosophy, religion and some popular science.

185

Thus the range of titles reproduced in large print for the partially sighted has grown steadily. By 1966 two hundred books were listed in the Ulverscroft catalogue, and in 1967 the Keith Jennison series numbered one hundred titles.

The reaction of the partially sighted to the large print format was, according to a questionnaire circulated by British public libraries for the LA '. . . divergent and sometimes contradictory'.[2] The Books for Readers with Defective Sight Sub-committee which had devised and issued the questionnaire, decided to direct some of the Nuffield Trust funds to a research project to examine the technical problems of large-print publishing. Alison Shaw was appointed as research associate to conduct the necessary investigation. She examined in detail the factors affecting the legibility of printed material. The results of her research, examined in more detail on pages 189-90 were published in 1969 as *Print for partial sight*.[3]

In the USA three years previously, Jack Prince of Ohio State University had begun work on a Library Technology Project for the American Library Association. The intention was to examine different type faces and type sizes to determine which would be the most appropriate for use in producing large print books for the partially sighted. The results of Dr Prince's research, it was hoped, would establish criteria which could act as a guide for publishers of large type material.

The problems of the partially sighted were now attracting the interest of librarians. A conference on the low-vision reader was held in Washington in 1965. The conference concluded that the books available for the adult partially sighted reader were completely inadequate. It was even more critical of the provisions made for children with severe sight defects which, the conference felt, were almost totally neglected. A meeting sponsored by the US Office of Education's Library Service Board, Office of Disadvantaged and Handicapped, examined the special reading difficulties of those with serious sight defects. In London, British librarians

held a conference in 1970 on print for the visually handicapped.

The needs of readers

There are several related questions: what are the special
reading needs of the visually handicapped? How can effective standards and specifications be formulated? What are
the most effective ways of providing an adequate supply of
books to the partially sighted?

Research into the factors which make print legible has
been in progress for a number of years. The obvious possibility to increase impact of print is to increase the size of the
type face. An early pioneer in the search for the most suitable type size for printing books for the partially sighted was
Robert B Irwin, who became the director of the American
Foundation for the Blind. While working to establish educational programmes for blind and partially sighted children,
Robert Irwin introduced printed works in thirty-six point
type for partially sighted children in the Cleveland public
schools in 1914. On the basis of this and other experiments
conducted between 1919 and 1920, Irwin established that
twenty-four point type was more readable. The relationship
of size to legibility was not completely established in these
early experiments. Later work tended to confirm that while
the use of a larger type face did increase legibility, it was not
possible to draw firm conclusions about the optimum size of
type for maximum legibility.

Other possibilities were also explored. Between 1928 and
1938 the National Institute for the Blind (UK) instituted a
series of studies of the reactions of teachers and children to
large print material. The children apparently preferred a
sans-serif face, Gill Sans Bold. The findings of these early
experiments were given substance by the work of Prince in the
USA and Shaw in the UK. Both were engaged in establishing
criteria for type legibility, and their conclusions have done
much to influence the presentation of large print publishing.

Dr Prince related his examination of print legibility to the reactions of the partially sighted living in institutions and homes in Ohio. The points which he considered were related to those elements which can contribute to type legibility: the optimum size, style, proportions, spacings between words and letters, length of lines and the contrast between paper and type.[4] The subsequent report recognised that there were differences between the reading levels and needs of the child with defective vision and the partially sighted adult. The young needed to be able to read printed material relevant to their education. The reasons for the older person's reading habits were not so clearly defined but they would, in some cases, read to compensate for a decline in physical activity. The child with an eye condition might hope for a complete or partial cure; for the elderly, apart from those with cataracts, there was no such prognostication.[5]

The conclusions reached by Dr Prince were that:

i) A type face of conventional design, such as Baskerville, could be successfully used for printing books for the partially sighted.

ii) The type used should have clean edges and those elements which contribute to the blurring of letterpress should be avoided.

iii) The type should be between sixteen and eighteen points in size, with the lower case o at least 2.7 mm in its vertical measurement, the ascenders and descenders to be not more than 17.5 per cent of the letter size.

iv) The length of the line should not extend beyond thirty-six picas.

v) The periods and commas should be bolder than those employed in conventionally printed books. Hyphenation should be kept to a minimum, and wherever possible, eliminated.[6]

Prince found that eighteen point type was the largest size which could be used. In practical terms, the larger the type, the fewer words on a page. This would, effectively, mean producing books larger than those printed by conventional type. An alternative would be to extend the line, but this introduced the possibility that the reader would find it difficult to encompass the meaning of sentences. Fewer words to a line would result in the reader constantly switching from the end of one line to the beginning of the next, making continuous reading difficult. It would also increase the number of hyphenations, with words at the end of the line being constantly broken. The use of excessively large print would make it difficult for the partially sighted reader to see more than one small section of the text at a time, which would militate against easy and continuous reading.[7]

The work of Alison Shaw on the whole reinforces the conclusions reached by Prince.[8] She stresses that the size of type used for printing is an important element in legibility. She confirms the finding that progressively increasing the size of type does not bring a corresponding increase in legibility.[9] Prince's view that it is necessary to distinguish between the needs of adults and children is substantiated by Shaw: adults, she found, could benefit from the provision of books in large print, but the size of type-face was not so significant for children with impaired vision, who were able to compensate for their deficiencies by bringing the book closer to their eyes.[10] This technique was not effective for the elderly.

The weight of type used was significant (weight in printing terminology signifying the boldness of the impression of the type upon the paper).[11] but, unlike Prince, she did not discern any appreciable benefits for children in the use of a sans serif face.[12] Variations in the spaces between words, letters or lines did not add significantly to legibility.[13]

Miss Shaw's final conclusion was that typographical factors were important in the provision of legible reading material for the partially sighted adult. An increase of thirty-five per cent in legibility could be achieved by improving typographical techniques.[14] She also noted that the degree of visual acuity retained by individuals bore no relation to the importance they ascribed to reading as an activity;

willpower, determination and the desire to read were more potent factors in the amount of reading undertaken.[15]

The publishers of large print books have been influenced by these findings. The majority of large-print material specially produced for the partially sighted has incorporated their proposals for typographical change. The face used in large print books is usually sixteen or eighteen point, and careful attention is usually paid to the weight and boldness of the face, with an attempt made to secure a sharp contrast between the printed material and the paper.

Large print publishers

In addition to Ulverscroft Books and the Austin Books already mentioned there are now a number of other British large print series available to the partially sighted reader. Cedric Chivers Ltd are working with the Reprints Sub-committee of the London and Home Counties branch of the Library Association to produce the New Portway Reprints Large Print Series, mainly of fiction. The Lythway Large Print Series consists predominantly of fiction works of the more popular kind: romantic, historical, mystery and crime novels. George Prior Publishers Ltd have issued over 180 titles in their large print series. Their books are virtually the same in size and weight as standard editions. Magna Print books, which are now being issued by Library Magna Book Ltd (Yorkshire), are concentrating upon works of practical interest: jam-making, wine-making, window-box-gardening. The titles in this range are made available by George Prior Associated Publishers.

Library provision

In the UK, the public library service has been the main agency for making large print material available to the partially sighted. While the output of the commercial publishers of books in large type face are available to the general public, in practice the majority of this material is acquired by public libraries.

The evolution of library provision for the partially sighted in the United States has followed a different path from that adopted in Britain. The requirement by Congress that its own library should accept responsibility for meeting the reading needs of all those unable to use books produced by conventional methods has been a crucial factor. The Division for the Blind and Physically Handicapped of the Library of Congress and its network of regional libraries makes no real distinction between the requirements of the visually and the physically handicapped reader.

The provision of books and related material to these same groups in the UK lacks this coordination. Public libraries have little concern with the provision of books to the blind, and the supply of books in braille or in recorded form is equally divided amongst a number of independent agencies. In spite of these limitations in the organisation of library services, the British public library has responded with commendable enthusiasm to its responsibilities. In 1971 sales of large print books to public libraries in Britain were greater than in other English-speaking countries. This has ensured a steady and assured sale for the specialists in large print publishing. The standard non-fiction work published by Ulverscroft will sell approximately 1300 copies depending upon the popularity of the author. General fiction sells between 1450 and 1500 copies.

The use made of large print books by the partially sighted reader is difficult to assess. Few public libraries place any restriction on the availability of this material and they can usually be borrowed by any member of the community. As the works in the large-print series are popular in content, the fully sighted will often select material from the large-print section of the library. This can give an exaggerated impression of the use made of this material.

Libraries do encounter difficulties in meeting the full reading needs of the partially sighted. Although there are a number of publishers now engaged in this special field, the range of titles available must inevitably compare unfavourably with the reading material which the rest of the community can draw upon. Indeed the blind person capable of reading braille has, in some circumstances, a greater choice of books than those with residual sight. In order to ensure sales, the publishers of large print books, have concentrated upon the production of popular works. Non-fiction which appears in large type format is limited to those subjects with a general appeal. Few, if any, specialist works are printed specifically for the partially sighted.

They may also encounter problems when borrowing large-print books, which are usually perceptibly larger than works printed in a type-face of more conventional size. As many partially sighted people are elderly they may experience difficulty in handling large-print books, and the act of lifting the books from the shelf and carrying them home has often been sufficiently taxing for the elderly reader to deter them from borrowing large print material again. The difficulty has been alleviated by Ulverscroft and other large print publishers changing the format of the works they publish. This has made the majority of large-print series easier to handle and to carry.

British public libraries do experience considerable difficulty in ensuring that the choice of titles in large-print is changed with sufficient regularity to maintain the interest of readers. This compares unfavourably to the position in the USA, where the users of material in large print can draw not only upon the resources of the regional libraries but also on the central organisation of the Department of Blind and Physically Handicapped Readers. The only alternative source of large print material which British public libraries can draw upon are the Austin Books made available by the National Library for the Blind. This is a series which provides a valuable supply of classic novels and other more advanced works, but it is not, unfortunately, as extensively advertised as it might be.

The increase in the number of commercial publishers willing to produce at least popular titles in large print indicates that for the forseeable future, at least, this form of publication will be available for the partially sighted reader. Any sudden rise in the cost of book production or a drastic cut in public expenditure (with a corresponding reduction in the financial support being given to libraries) could see this particularly vulnerable form of publishing compelled to limit its activities.

But the future of large print publishing could also be affected by other, related, developments. As has been pointed out in the previous chapter, there have been a number of technical advances in the presentation of books in recorded form. Books on tape or disc are now available from a number of agencies. Whereas the policy of the Division for the Blind and Physically Handicapped of the Library of Congress has been to make no distinction between the reading needs of the blind and the partially sighted, the demands made by the blind upon the Talking Book Service in the United Kingdom preclude it being extended to the partially sighted. However, other talking book services in the UK (see page 162) do not distinguish between the blind and the physically handicapped when defining their readership.

For those who are suffering severely from deficient sight, the talking book is an effective method of enjoying literature, but the costs of talking book production are higher than those for the large print series. Books on tape or disc need relatively expensive playback equipment. There is an additional problem that as the use of tape or disc for the production of books for the partially sighted is becoming more widespread, publishers may become reluctant to give permission for their books to be reproduced in this way without some form of recompense. This situation exists in a number of countries where approval has to be obtained for the recording of each individual title.

An alternative possibility for making books available is the magnification aid. There have, in recent years, been a number of attempts made to produce an efficient magnifier for the use of the partially sighted. Some of these aids are now being produced commercially and they range from simple hand lenses to highly sophisticated systems.

A number of hand held magnifiers have been developed specifically for reading printed material. They are usually rectangular in shape and sufficiently large enough to encompass a reasonable reading area. The handle may be angled from the lens to enable the arm to be rested on the table while reading. Magnifiers on stands are also available, these being particularly helpful for the reader suffering from other physical handicaps. Some magnifiers are equipped with a light which can be focused on the page. They may also be fitted with a jointed arm to enable the light and the reading lens to be adjusted to a comfortable position. There are also magnifiers designed to read one line of type at a time, these are usually known as strip magnifiers.

The cost of providing such equipment is considerable and few libraries will be willing to incur the necessary expenditure. Academic libraries, where readers are working on the premises for a long period, may consider that the purchase of an adjustable magnifier on a stand will be justified. This could be of assistance not only to the student or teacher with partial vision, but also to the fully sighted person for close work. But there are limitations inherent in the use of magnification aids for reading purposes, some of which are summarised here:

i) Hand lenses can be heavy and awkward to use, and this can make reading over a long period very tiring for the elderly and physically handicapped.

ii) Magnifying aids can be difficult to hold steady over a page of type.

iii) There will be some optical distortion at the edges of the lens.

iv) The limited area which can be seen through the lens makes speedy and continuous reading difficult.

v) In order to read with the use of a magnifying aid a book must be laid flat, and this introduces two difficulties: either the reader will have to bend over the book, which can be tiring; or the books will not lie flat, making it difficult to hold a constant image through the lens.

vi) The lens can distort the pattern of light on the page.

Although more advanced reading aids have largely eliminated problems such as these, the costs of purchasing the better magnifying equipment have deterred the majority of libraries from making such provision. Certainly there is a need for an effective, inexpensive magnification aid for the partially sighted.

Other methods are being examined, not only to meet the requirements of those with impaired vision but also those who have other physical disabilities. Currently experiments are being made exploring the potentialities of books printed as scrolls. For the visually handicapped with other physical disabilities, the Saltus Corporation of Massachusetts has introduced their reading system, consisting of a case weighing about eighteen pounds into which the 'book' is loaded. The reading matter can be seen through a 'window' measuring 22 x 29 cm (9 x 11 inches). The books used by the Saltus system are printed on scrolls in a large type face. They fit into the machine and can be read through the screen as the scroll revolves. The scroll can be turned both forwards and backwards, and for the severely handicapped there is a mouth control which can be operated by the tongue, lips or chin. For those with severely impaired vision, a magnifying lens can be fitted.

There are six hundred titles available through the Saltus Book Club with an emphasis upon recreational reading. There is also however a reasonably wide selection of non-fiction for adults and the series includes children's books. Nor are the potentialities confined to the handicapped. The system can be used to assist those with learning problems, and the machine can be fitted with a roll of blank paper upon which a child can write or draw.

It is perhaps too early to assess the significance of the Saltus Reading System for libraries. The machine is expensive, and the scrolls are, as yet, available only through the book club. Clearly the system has potential; and libraries could certainly utilise it if a commercial agreement was reached and the resources made available.

REFERENCES
1 Fitzgerald, Roy G 'Reactions to blindness: an exploratory study of adults with recent loss of sight' in *The handicapped person in the community: a reader and a source book* (ed) David M Boswell and Janet M Wingrove. London, Tavistock Publications, 1974, 281.

2 Library Association Research and Development Committee: Books for Readers with Defective Sight Sub-committee *Memorandum of evidence to the Department of Education and Science, Committee on the Education of the Visually Handicapped* 1969, 2.

3 Shaw, Alison *Print for partial sight* Report to the Library Association Sub-committee on Books for Readers with Defective Sight. London, Library Association, 1969.

4 Prince, J H 'Printing for the visually handicapped' *Journal of typographical research* 1(1), January 1967, 31.

5 Ibid 32.

6 Ibid 45-46.

7 Ibid 46.

8 Shaw op cit.

9 Ibid 23, 57-60.

10 Ibid 59-60.

11 Ibid 23, 60.

12 Ibid 23, 60-61.

13 Ibid 61.

14 Ibid 65.

15 Ibid 63.

NINE

LIBRARY SERVICES
FOR THE MENTALLY SUBNORMAL

THE PROVISION of library facilities designed to meet the special difficulties of the mentally subnormal (MSN) is a comparatively recent development. The reasons for this neglect are similar to those which have contributed to the general disinterest in the reading needs of the physically handicapped. There is a lack of awareness, amongst librarians, of the value of reading in helping the mentally subnormal extend their capabilities. And in the past, specialists working with the subnormal have displayed little support for the introduction of proper library facilities into their institutions.

Those improvements which have been made in the quality of library provision owe much to the advances which have been made in the education and training of those with severe mental retardation. This, coupled with more enlightened attitudes towards the mentally subnormal, has led to the emigrance of library programmes for this hitherto neglected group. Librarians are demonstrating that they can assist with the education and rehabilitation work which is being done with such patients. As yet, however, this participation has been confined to the relatively few institutions which have appointed a full-time, qualified librarian. The special facilities which have been·formulated by public libraries for other handicapped sections of the community have not been developed on the same scale for the mentally subnormal.

The term 'mentally handicapped' can embrace conditions of mental subnormality, mental retardation and mental deficiency. Certain mental disorders are more prevalent than others: approximately one third of the children in schools for the mentally subnormal are suffering from Down's Syndrome (mongolism).

Several attempts have been made to classify the mentally subnormal, using Intelligence Quotient (IQ) Scales. The World Health Organisation has arrived at the following table:

mild mental handicap	IQ 52-56
moderate mental handicap	IQ 36-51
severe mental handicap	IQ 20-35
profound mental handicap	IQ minus 20.

Such categorisation is subject to error and any IQ assessment has to be related to other factors which can influence the score; in a multi-racial society, those drawn from the ethnic minorities may be at a disadvantage because the tests make certain cultural assumptions. Equally, the available evidence suggests that growing up in an economically deprived home can have an effect upon a child's language development. This would also affect the capacity of an individual to deal effectively with intelligence tests.

There are other sound reasons for treating intelligence tests with caution. The measurement of intelligence is a far from exact science and experts differ in their opinions of the respective effectiveness and accuracy of the IQ tests currently in use. It is unlikely that librarians will be directly concerned with the application of IQ tests to the mentally subnormal. They should, nevertheless, be aware of the strengths and limitations of the different testing techniques if they are offering a library service to the mentally handicapped. They will in such circumstances need to be capable of relating the results of such tests to the reading material appropriate to the patient's capabilities.

The intelligence testing methods introduced by the Frenchmen Alfred Binet and Theophile Simon in 1905 represent the beginnings of the systematic assessment of the mental capacity of the intellectually retarded. The results of their research were used to devise the Binet-Simon Scale. This test was further refined, in 1916, by Lewis Terman, an American working at Stanford University, the new system being called the Stanford-Binet intelligence test.

The reliability of the scales introduced by Binet has been questioned, but with its later derivatives the scale can be of value in determining the intelligence of slow learners. A series of extensively-used tests are based upon the Wechsler Adult Intelligence Scale (WAIS) and the Wechsler Intelligence Scale for Children (WISC). These are inspired by Wechsler's theory that the aggregate of an individual's intelligence is their ability to relate to their environment, their capacity to act in a rational manner and their determination to direct their actions purposefully. The WAIS and related tests have the merit that they do allow for the influences of a person's cultural and social background.

It is especially difficult to measure the intelligence of those suffering from visual, speech or hearing disabilities. There are IQ tests which are suitable for testing the intelligence of those who have sensory or physical disabilities. The Ravens Progressive Matrices consists of a booklet with a series of pages each with a pattern printed on it. A piece of the pattern is missing and below it will be a choice of designs, one of which is appropriate to the missing piece. The child is expected to select the right piece. For the auditorally impaired child without verbal skills this can be done by pointing. The Wechsler Intelligence Scale for Children is appropriate for determining the IQ of children between five and sixteen, who are deaf or partially deaf. The WISC has both verbal and non-verbal scales, which can give some indication of the effect which hearing impairment has had upon the child's learning capacity. The tests consist of picture completion, picture arrangement, and the ordering of either numbers or letters. Another testing technique, the Snijders-Oomen Test, is for children in the same age group. This was devised in Holland and it is now used in the United Kingdom to assess the mental capacity of hearing-impaired children.

Institutional library services

It was suggested earlier that the emergence of library services to the mentally subnormal has been linked to the growth of rehabilitation programmes in schools and centres for the mentally subnormal. While this is a valid observation, it would be equally true to suggest that librarians have had to proceed empirically in determining the precise contribution which they can make to the education of the mentally retarded. There is a paucity of reading material suitable for the adult mentally subnormal patient which has made it difficult to establish appropriate collections for this group. Librarians have needed to look beyond traditional library resources in order to build up collections with items which will be of use to the mentally subnormal.

In establishing a service for the residents of an institution, the librarian needs to be aware of the differing capabilities of the potential readership. F William Happ has noted that there will, normally, be three main categories of the subnormal in an institution: the educable, with an IQ of 50-75; the trainable, with an IQ of 25-49; and the custodial, with an IQ of less than 25. This last group, he feels, will be outside the province of the library service because of their low mental capabilities.[1]

There are other factors which affect the ability to use reading materials. The patient may be suffering from physical or emotional problems which reduce the capacity to learn, to read or to write. He or she might be subject to uncontrollable fits, or they may have other disabilities including visual or auditory handicaps. Despite these difficulties it will often be possible for the educable mentally subnormal patient to acquire certain skills—to read, write, and absorb some knowledge of basic subjects. The majority of educable subnormal individuals can be trained to a level sufficient for them to undertake unskilled or semi-skilled employment. The trainable can be taught to care for themselves, to acquire acceptable social skills and sufficient powers of perception to fit them for unskilled employment in a sheltered workshop.

The fundamental aims of mental institutions will help to clarify the role of the librarian in such an establishment. Charles H Hallas has summarised the purpose of these institutions as follows:

i) To assist the inmate to lead an enjoyable life within the institution.

ii) To help and direct the formation of good habits and positive attitudes.

iii) To bring out individual aptitudes and abilities, to stimulate interests relevant to these attributes.

iv) To develop potential working proficiency.

v) To encourage the inmates to think for themselves and become more independent.[2]

For the educable and trainable, the ultimate intention of the staff of an institution will be to fit the individual for life in the community. The librarian will direct the resources and activities of the library towards this goal. Teachers of the educable mental retardee of school age will find books and magazines with simple vocabulary valuable as adjuncts to the instruction they are giving. Reading material can be useful for strengthening the child's knowledge, improving reading skills as well as providing a source of entertainment.

Happ's survey into the reading habits and interests of mentally subnormal children found that the educable retardee between the ages of twelve and eighteen enjoyed many of the topics popular with general public library users. The books in most demand included romantic novels, mysteries, westerns and adventure stories. Books with sporting and historical themes, and those which dealt with biology in a simple fashion were much sought after. Happ stresses that although such a youngster may have a low reading age, interests will be appropriate to real age. Given the right type of reading material the educable young person will become an enthusiastic reader.[3]

The adult educable retarded person will normally reject attempts to press children's books upon him. If the library is to make an effective contribution in an adult institution or centre, it has to supply reading material with simple vocabulary but adult interest level. The trainable mentally subnormal generally enjoy looking at pictures, and the majority will be capable of identifying the essential characteristics of uncomplicated pictures. They will also be able to identify sizes, shapes and colours. Books and magazines which are profusely illustrated, and with text confined to a minimum, should therefore be available. The text of books will be of little importance as the patient may well lack reading skills. Books which present simple stories in picture form, perhaps with simple vocabulary in large print, will be sufficient. The topics in the works chosen should reflect everyday themes, as the patient in this category is unlikely to be able to grasp abstract ideas.

For the educable retardee, (who is likely to be capable of working), reading material which is designed to exemplify situations which will be encountered at work will be of help. Books which stress the value of a clean appearance, getting to work on time and how to work with others, will give the essential background information. Those works which can demonstrate these concepts will support the education and rehabilitation work taking place in the institution.

An example of reading material produced specifically for the mentally handicapped child are the 'Clumsy Charlie' reading books. This series is valuable for teaching the child necessary social skills, including interaction with others and the rights of friends and relatives. Titles issued in this series include *Clumsy Charlie at home, Clumsy Charlie at work, Clumsy Charlie at large* and *Clumsy Charlie out and about*. The principal character in the series is someone with whom the retarded child can identify. The situations which Charlie encounters are presented humorously, but with an appropriate solution. The conclusions drawn are intended to help the reader understand social attitudes and to live effectively in the community.

A similar series is the 'Gunzberg' books, which cover those problems which the mentally subnormal person might encounter in social situations, for example *Trouble at work*. There are several sets of books which are intended for slow, reluctant or retarded readers which may also be suitable for the mentally retarded. Ladybird publish a number of series intended for the backward reader, some of which could be used to teach the mentally subnormal child to read. Ladybird reading kits are specifically intended to help the educationally subnormal to acquire basic reading skills. Benn have introduced a series 'Inner ring hipsters' with a teenage reading interest but with a reading age of seven or eight. There are two series: 'Red circle hipsters' by Richard Parker, which centres upon four English children whilst the 'Green circle hipsters', by Clive King, portrays Rima, a young Asian girl, and her brother Sami. 'Inner ring sports' cover the more popular games with appropriate titles: *Goalie, Splash, Top spin*. The Inner ring series does have a wider appeal than to those who are suffering from mental handicap, but the simple illustrations and clear text do make them very suitable for work with mental retardees.

Franklin Watts 'Let's go' series has certain helpful features for the educable, although, again, they are designed for a larger audience. The series covers everyday situations: *The garage, The shops, The railway station*. Each page has a coloured illustration with the text kept to a minimum. New words, relevant to each book, are printed in bold face type. The illustrations are photographs taken in the situations appropriate to each theme.

The librarian providing a service to the mentally subnormal should scan the many series of books published for the slow learner. In many cases these will be too advanced, requiring an extensive vocabulary and dealing with situations which are too complex for the mental retardee to comprehend. Nevertheless, those series which cover everyday happenings, which are well illustrated and use simple, clearly printed words, will be especially helpful to the educable retardee. The trainable retardee too may derive some pleasure from the elementary reading books.

The library in an institution will need to acquire non-book materials to support the educational work of the establishment. Music in recorded, as well as printed form, can be used to help educate in a variety of verbal and physical skills. It can be used to assist singing sessions which are held in the institution. In addition to providing the patients with a great deal of pleasure, relaxation and amusement, there are additional benefits from singing which have been identified by Happ:[4]

i) It enables the patient to use and listen to words and sequences of words and these can be learnt by heart.

ii) It can provide an introduction to a wide range of concepts and objects including colour, animals, countries and events.

iii) It will be a means of learning rhythm.

Singing can be accompanied by clapping in time to the music, or the children can use simple hand movements. This is valuable in learning physical coordination as well as inculcating a sense of rhythm.

The educable mentally subnormal will be capable of learning to play simple tunes on musical instruments such as drums or cymbals. The librarian should ensure that musical scores of simple tunes are available if the use of musical instruments is taught in the establishment.

The library should contain a selection of music on tape and disc, this being chosen with the assistance of the medical and therapeutical staff. The emphasis will be upon songs and tunes with a simple, repetitive beat. The words of the song should be easy to learn and they should be repeated frequently throughout.

Happ suggests that where the music is without words the rhythms can be more complex as the patients will be able to concentrate upon one aspect of the song. Pop groups which play music with a strong beat are noticeably popular with the educable. Happ goes on to explore the possibility that music can profitably be related to the emotional state of the retarded child. Those children who are hyperactive will benefit from listening to more relaxing music and will often respond better to those forms of music with a less insistent note.[5]

Visual aids of all kinds can be important educational media in an institution for the subnormal. There will be some multi-handicapped mental retardees, some with visual and auditory handicaps, who will not be able to benefit from the use of visual aids. The others will often be able to derive both entertainment and information from films, film-strips and slides. For the educable, the choice of films and film-strips should be as generous as that available to the rest of the community. The only restriction to be observed will be that the form of presentation should be as uncomplicated as possible. The length of the film should also be carefully monitored: the concentration of even an educable patient rarely extends beyond half-an-hour.

The trainable mentally retarded enjoys short film-strips and slides, especially those which deal with themes and situations with which they can identify. Happ says that they are unlikely to comprehend films, and their lack of ability to conceptualise and their slow speed of comprehension make it difficult for them to enjoy this medium.[6]

The severely mentally subnormal (SMSN) will be unlikely to respond even to the most carefully-selected reading or audio-visual material. The training which those with an IQ of 25 or less are receiving will be concentrated almost entirely upon basic handling and sensory skills. This will be given with the aid of material rarely included in the stock of a traditional library. Items such as peg-boards, buttons of different shapes and sizes, simple puzzles, paper to cut out, toys which are strong and washable will all have their place in training. The purpose of this is to give the severely handicapped an opportunity to acquire a sense of touch and also to develop their coordination techniques by feeling objects of different sizes, shapes and weights.

It might be questioned whether librarians should have the responsibility for acquiring and storing material of this kind.

The therapists and the teachers, it could be argued, are the proper workers to control the materials which they need for their classes, and that librarians lack the necessary background, education and training to work effectively with this type of patient. Many of the severely mentally subnormal will be confined to their beds, without even the most basic control of their bodies, and books and other forms of publication traditionally assembled by libraries have little significance for those in this condition.

Arguments of this kind are difficult to refute, for the severely mentally subnormal do require highly trained, dedicated help. Nevertheless librarians can help both the patients and those who work with them by offering the resources of a properly administered library. The collection, organisation and distribution of reading and other materials is within the province of librarianship. Public and school libraries are going beyond the conventional collecting policies of the past in assembling artefacts including games and toys for slow learners and other disadvantaged sections of society. It would seem a logical progression for the library in a school or training centre for the subnormal to collect and disseminate anything which supports the educational and rehabilitation programmes of such establishments.

Roslyn Taffel has provided a description of the work of the Royal Palm School library.[7] This is an educational establishment for the education of 'special children', a category which embraces the mentally retarded. The introduction of the federal Elementary Secondary Education Act provided the opportunity for the appointment of a full-time librarian to the school. The librarian, working closely with the teaching staff, has introduced programmes of library activities including story-telling and reading-aloud sessions. The teachers have been persuaded to tape-record stories which have been played in the library to the children.

The children in the school have been encouraged to work in the library, issuing books, straightening the shelves and repairing books. In some cases the more advanced children have been allowed to help others in their choice of books. The rules and procedures of the library have been established by experience and they are adapted to the needs of the children.

In those institutions for the adult mentally subnormal, programmes of education in academic subjects will naturally occupy a less significant place. However, if the adult can be taught to read and write, the benefits will be considerable. To supplement the basic reading courses which patients are receiving, the library can provide a selection of easy-to-read books of adult interest.

The library, in an institution for the mentally retarded must be, above all, a place where the inmate can feel welcome. It must be a place where they can find enjoyment and relaxation. For those who anticipate returning to the community, a pleasant recollection of the library will be an incentive to seek the same opportunities in the local public library.

Public library services to the mentally subnormal
The literature of librarianship contains few references to the participation by the public library in the provision of literature to the mentally subnormal. Such innovations that have been made are largely confined to making special provision for the subnormal child. The majority of public librarians would seem to subscribe to the view that the mentally subnormal, with their limited reading skills, are incapable of deriving any benefit from access to all but the simplest of reading material. Recently, however, some public libraries have been responding to requests for assistance from institutions for the mentally subnormal. An example of the willingness of public libraries to explore the possibilities of developing such programmes is provided by the work of the Beverley Heights (New Jersey) Public Library.[8] This opportunity came when the director of a neighbouring institution for the mentally retarded adult, the Independent Living

Center of the John E Runnells Hospital, approached the Beverley Heights librarian.

The librarian was asked if selected groups of the mentally retarded from the institution could be allowed to visit the library. A programme was arranged, with the library staff arranging a series of events for each group. These included, amongst other things, selected film-shows. In cooperation with the center, the staff of the library made a film, 'A day at the Independent Living Center'. The purpose of the film, which was supported by the New Jersey State Library, was to publicise the work of the center. There was, too, the associated intention of making the community more aware of the problems of the mentally subnormal.

As part of this programme, a number of tapes were made as instructional aids for the mentally subnormal. These include such practical topics as sandwich making, tidying beds and other activities centred upon the home. Helen Montgomery, the former director of the Beverley Heights Library, feels that the visits to the library gave the mental retardees the opportunity to enjoy a normal, everyday activity. It also made them aware of the library, both as an educational and a social institution. Those with some reading ability were encouraged to join the library and borrow material. The visitors did borrow a variety of items: film-strips, tapes, records and paintings.

This work, plus that of a few other public libraries, does indicate that there is a role for the development of reading programmes for at least the educable mentally subnormal individual. Modern medical practice is to encourage the retardee to live as normal a life as possible in the community. This is creating a climate which is encouraging public libraries to formulate new policies towards the provision of services for the mentally handicapped. Peter Mittler has argued that properly planned, systematic education and training can do much to help the mentally handicapped to lead happy, useful lives.[9] This training should begin at birth and proceed beyond school leaving age. If these views are accepted, then the public library certainly has a part to play.

One possibility is for the public library to act as an information centre on the prevention of mental handicap. Current research indicates that many cases of mental subnormality could have been prevented. If the public were more aware of the dangers to unborn children they could take steps to avoid them. This information would embrace the effects upon the foetus of certain illnesses such as rubella, the damage caused to the unborn child by excessive drinking and smoking, the hazards associated with certain drugs and medical treatment. The approval of the medical profession would have to be sought before public libraries acted as centres for public education in the causes of mental subnormality, for librarians would not wish to appear as though they were encouraging the public to diagnose their health conditions. However, the supply of information on preventive medicine is a rather different matter. Public libraries, in cooperation with public health authorities, can do much to alert the public to the causes of mental retardation. This would require a change in the attitude of many professional librarians. The traditional approach of public librarians to the provision of medical literature is one of caution. While this approach has something to recommend it, there is the possibility that excessive timidity could discourage librarians from performing a valuable public service.

A family with a mentally subnormal child will be confronted with many daunting practical and social problems. The public library can again act as a resource centre, providing literature on the more common forms of mental subnormality. The leaflets issued by central and local government and other health organisations on the facilities and opportunities for the mentally subnormal should be systematically collected. The public library can also act as a referral centre for the mentally disabled, directing them to the institution or centre which can best assist them.

If there are pre-school educational programmes for the mentally subnormal, the public library can support this work by acquiring books and other material relevant to the classes being held. This can be linked to a series of regular visits to the library by handicapped children with their teachers.

In the United Kingdom, developments in the past decade have centred upon the provision of opportunities for employment of the mentally subnormal. These job opportunities owe much to the work of Adult Training Centres, Employment Rehabilitation Centres and the efforts of Disablement Resettlement Officers. In addition to the creation of work opportunities, these agencies have introduced educational and vocational training programmes at their centres. The training courses for the adult mental retardee teach basic reading and numeracy skills. There is an emphasis too upon practical training: crafts, cooking, self-care and economic self-sufficiency. The British public library, as yet, has made little attempt to cater for the possibilities offered by the appearance of courses of this kind. Peter Mittler[10] feels that it is essential that the mentally retarded individual be given the opportunity to visit the establishments provided by local authorities. These, he suggests, would include colleges, sports and leisure centres and clubs. Public libraries should form part of this itinerary.

REFERENCES

1 Happ, F William 'Multi-media services for retardees in institutions' Top of the news 25(3), April 1969, 268.

2 Hallas, Charles H The care and training of the mentally subnormal 3rd ed Bristol, Wright and Sons, 1967.

3 Happ op cit, 271.

4 Happ op cit, 269-270, 271.

5 Happ op cit, 270.

6 Happ op cit, 270.

7 Taffel, Roslyn 'The Royal Palm School Library' Top of the news 25(3), April 1969, 279-281.

8 Montgomery, Helen 'Special report: outreach to the retarded' Wilson Library bulletin 50(9), May 1976, 688-690.

9 Mittler, Peter 'Outline of a mental handicap service' Residential social work 17(1), January 1977, 4-9.

10 Ibid 8.

TEN

LIBRARY SERVICES FOR THE DEAF

THE PREVIOUS CHAPTER sought to emphasise the neglect of the reading requirements of the mentally subnormal. Recognition by libraries of the special reading problems of the deaf has been equally tardy. The assumption has been that the deaf do not have any difficulties in using the normal services and facilities of a library. There is too, a general ignorance of the nature of deafness and the problems of communication with others which it brings.

There are a number of categories of deafness. The term 'deaf' itself is used to indicate a hearing loss in the 'better' ear, severe enough for the sufferer to be unable to distinguish speech even—in the more extreme cases—with the assistance of a hearing aid. 'Hard-of-hearing' implies a hearing loss sufficient to effect the perception of conversational speech, but with sufficient residual hearing to comprehend the spoken word under optimum conditions, either with or without a hearing-aid. 'Hearing-impaired' covers all degrees of deafness, irrespective of the severity of hearing loss or of the cause of the deafness.

The condition of deafness is subject to a number of variables: the age at which deafness strikes; the speed with which the loss of hearing progresses; and the presence of other, sometimes related, handicaps. Those who are born deaf, or become deaf in early childhood, suffer the severest disadvantage. The profoundly deaf child, unable to hear since birth, will not develop language skills without some form of special education. Even with the aid of a specifically devised programme, the deaf child will often lag

211

behind the development of contemporaries with unimpaired hearing. The child with average hearing will have developed a vocabulary of around five thousand words by the age of five, and the acquisition of this vocabulary will have been supported by the formation of a body of general knowledge upon which school work can be based. The deaf child at five, unless he or she has received some pre-school teaching, will have a limited vocabulary and poor communication skills.

The education of the deaf has, for some years, been complicated by the controversy which has centred upon the use of hand signs for verbal communication. In both Europe and America, the dispute has been between the advocates of 'oralism' and 'manualism'. Oralism is based upon the use of residual hearing, lip-reading and also the written word to communicate with others. Manualism implies that the deaf person will rely more upon the use of hand signs and finger spelling for speaking to other deaf persons and to the hearing who have the same skills. The differences of opinion which exist between the supporters of the two systems will not directly concern librarians, but it could influence the sort of special provision which might be made for the deaf reader.

Whichever system is taught, the disadvantages encountered by the deaf child often persist throughout its life. It is estimated that sixty per cent of deaf school leavers in the United Kingdom have a reading age of less than eight. In the United States, thirty per cent of deaf students over the age of sixteen are functionally illiterate. Their prospects of employment are correspondingly reduced.

These problems will not be so acute for those who become deaf later in life. They will have acquired the ability to speak intelligibly, and their education will have been completed. Nevertheless deafness, at any age, can bring profound difficulties. For those who are still working there will be an increasing inability to communicate with colleagues, and in those occupations which bring frequent contact with the public, the loss of efficiency may result in the loss of employment. Deafness is a complaint which often accompanies the process of growing old, and to the elderly person who may already be suffering from a lack of contact with others, the loss of hearing may increase the feeling of isolation.

The library and the deaf
Staff training:

If the deaf are to be encouraged to use a library, the staff will need to be aware of their special problems. The library staff should, ideally, be trained to use the correct techniques in speaking to those who have impaired hearing. A widely-held and quite erroneous impression is that hearing-aids automatically enable the deaf to hear clearly. Hearing-aids merely amplify sounds, with the result that background noises too are exaggerated. This can make it difficult for the deaf person relying on a hearing-aid to distinguish what is being said. Children, in particular, find that such aids are not always of much assistance.

If there is a staff training programme for helping the deaf library user, it should deal with the special difficulties of those who have been profoundly deaf since birth. Sufferers will have learnt the meanings of vocal sounds by imitating lip movements or by vibration techniques, and in some cases those who are born profoundly deaf are never able to formulate words in a manner intelligible to the general public. When speaking to such a reader, the member of staff should face the deaf person, form each word separately with proper lip movements, and speak slowly. Above all there must be a firm training to avoid any show of irritation or loss of patience.

Many deaf people will have been trained to lipread. In their training library staff should be informed of the strengths and weaknesses of lipreading techniques. Between forty and sixty per cent of words in the English language are homophoneous, having the same speech movements for different words (eg mat, bat, pat). As many do not enunciate clearly,

213

the deaf person is often at a loss to identify the words being used. Optimum conditions for lipreading require a good speaker, adequate lighting, with the speaker directly facing the listener, preferably singly and not in a group. Even in these conditions it may only be possible for the deaf person relying upon speech reading to comprehend twenty-five per cent of what is being said. If speakers constantly turn their heads or use imprecise lip movements, then the level of understanding can fall sharply. Even a thick moustache can make the wearer incomprehensible to someone attempting to lipread.

Information and referral services for the deaf:
The possibilities of public libraries developing special information and referral services for the physically handicapped have already been discussed. In general, the same provision should be made for the deaf patron. There are other facilities specifically relevant to the problems of the hearing-impaired. The library could collect trade and professional literature on hearing aids, maintaining lists of reputable audiologists and suppliers. The book collections should contain material which can help the deaf with their problems: manuals of lipreading and finger spelling should be available.

Employment of the deaf:
The nature of library work does require that a member of the staff, regularly dealing with the public, should be able to communicate freely without physical impediment. If there are any staff hard of hearing whose difficulties can be corrected by an aid, they should be given the same work opportunities as their fully-hearing colleagues. The profoundly deaf, too, can work effectively in the non-public departments of a library.

Every encouragement should be given to the hearing-impaired to apply for library posts, and there are indications that libraries are considering their responsibilities towards the deaf more sympathetically. The Library of Congress is providing an example of ways in which the deaf can be successfully employed. The Processing Department currently employs twenty deaf persons, and the other six departments of the library have their complement of hearing-impaired staff. To improve the work environment the library has introduced a course for its staff to learn sign language. The programme was established with the assistance of an instructor from the Gallaudet College in Washington, which is a liberal arts college for the deaf. The purpose of the course is to facilitate communication between the hearing and deaf members of the library staff, and to improve the service given to the deaf patrons. The Processing Department also has an MCM communications system. This is a teletypewriter which operates identically to normal telephone equipment except that the conversations are typed rather than spoken. The MCM teletypewriters work by dialing the number, then placing the telephone receiver in a special receptacle. Conversations, as they are typed out, appear on a screen.

Special provision for the deaf:
Persons who have become deaf later in life may not require separate library provision. For the most part they will use the same range of books and services which are available to the entire community. There are, nevertheless, certain possibilities for improving the library service to deaf patrons which have been created by the latest technological advances. The teletypewriter (TTY) has already been mentioned, and given that a growing number of the deaf may have TTY fitted into their homes, public libraries might consider installing one if there are sufficient numbers of deaf library users. This would give the deaf person the same access to the library as other members of society, and he or she would be able to reserve or renew books and request information by this means. Akron Summit County (Ohio) Public Library has introduced a TTY service for deaf patrons:

the library has a telephone connected to a TTY machine which can be used by the 150 deaf persons in the county who have teletypewriters in their homes.

There is need for libraries of all kinds to consider training one or more members of their staff in manual communication techniques. At present there are several systems of sign language in use. The official British and American systems of manual sign language are widely used; the Paget-Gorman systematic sign language, the Rochester method and the Cued Speech system all have their advocates. The system taught to the library staff will naturally be that which is used locally.

One possibility is to have a story hour for children both deaf and hearing, with the spoken narrative being accompanied by hand signs. Similarly talks on topics of interest to the adult deaf can be presented with the spoken word interpreted simultaneously into hand signs.

Children who have been profoundly deaf since birth may, as has been stated, experience difficulties with basic education. The library can assist by the provision of material which can assist in learning problems. This might include: easy reading books, alphabets on cards, non-book material, such as toys and games.

Library design:

The Gallaudet College for the Deaf has incorporated several unique features into the design of its library, to make it more suitable for the needs of the deaf student. While these innovations are not all appropriate for a library serving the general public, there are still possibilities for making the environment of a library more welcoming for the deaf patron. Some of the features discussed in the section on designing the library for the disabled (see page 131) will be equally helpful for the deaf. The use of carpets for floor covering instead of tiles can reduce the noise level and make it easier for the hard of hearing to understand what is being said to them. Any other precautions which reduce the amount of noise in the library will be similarly beneficial. Noisy equipment should, whenever possible, be operated in non-public rooms, and staff should be encouraged to work as quietly as possible.

The siting of the circulation and enquiry desks is important. Ideally they should be away from a busy street to avoid traffic noise, preferably they should not be located under low balconies which can muffle and possibly distort conversations. The guides and signs to the various departments and services should be as clear as possible, enabling the deaf person to find the facilities needed without asking the staff. A safety precaution would be to have flashing lights as a fire warning in addition to the usual bells.

SELECT READING LIST

GENERAL
Books and pamphlets
Casey, Genevieve M (compiler) *Libraries in the therapeutic society* Chicago, ALA, 1971.

Childers, Thomas *The information poor in America* Metuchen (NJ), Scarecrow Press, 1975.

Going, Mona E (editor) *Hospital libraries and work with the disabled* 2nd ed, London, LA, 1973.

Lewis, M Joy *Libraries for the handicapped: 1967 Sevensma prize essay* London, LA, 1969 (LA pamphlet 33).

Library Association, Hospital Libraries and Handicapped Readers Group *Libraries and therapy: papers given at the Hospital Libraries and Handicapped Readers Group Conference, Cambridge, 1967* London, the Group, 1968.

Library Association, Hospital Libraries and Handicapped Readers Group *Libraries for health and welfare* London, LA, 1971.

Martin, William (editor) *Library services to the disadvantaged* London, Bingley; Hamden, Conn, Linnet, 1975.

Periodical articles
American Library Association, Library Administrative Division 'Guide line for using volunteers in libraries' *American librarian* 2(4), April 1971, 407-408.

Casey, Genevieve M 'Library services to the handicapped and the institutionalized' *Library trends* 20(2), October 1971, 350-366.

Casey, Genevieve M 'Services to the disadvantaged' *Library trends* 23(2) October 1974, 271-285.

Douglass, H H 'Library services for the sick and handicapped: do we care enough? in *Proceedings, papers and summaries of discussions at the Public Library Conference held at Eastbourne, 15th-18th September 1975* London, LA, 1975, 27-31.

Drennan, Henry T 'Library legislation discovered' *Library trends* 24(1), July 1975, 115-133.

Going, Mona E 'Hospital libraries and libraries for readers with special needs' in: Sewell, P H (editor) *Five years' work in librarianship, 1961-1965* London, LA, 1968, 190-212.

'Library services to the disadvantaged' *Catholic library world* 45(9), April 1974, 420-445. (Special issue with articles on the mentally retarded, deaf children, prison libraries and other topics.)

Lovejoy, Eunice (editor) 'Library service for the blind and physically handicapped' *Health and Rehabilitative Library Services Division journal* 2(2), fall 1976, 2-19. (An issue which concentrates on some of the reading and information needs of the handicapped.)

Lucioli, C 'Minority of minorities: library service for the handicapped' *AHIL quarterly* 10 summer 1970, 42-45.

Lyman, Helen Huguenor (issue editor) 'Library programs and services to the disadvantaged' *Library trends* 20(2), October 1971, 187-471. (Issue devoted to library services to the ethnically, socially and physically handicapped.)

Phinney, Eleanor 'Recognising the institutional libraries: two decisive decades' *American librarian* 3(7), July/August 1972, 735-742.

HOSPITAL LIBRARIES

Books and pamphlets

American Library Association, Association of Hospital and Institution Libraries, Hospital Library Standards Committee *Standards for library services in health care institutions* Chicago, ALA, 1967.

Bloomquist, H J and others *Library practice in hospitals: a basic guide* Cleveland, Press of Case Western Reserve University, 1972.

Library Association *Hospital libraries: recommended standards for libraries in hospitals, 1972* London, LA, 1972.

Phinney, Eleanor (editor) *The library and the patient: an introduction to library services for patients in health care institutions* Chicago, ALA, 1977.

Pritchard, Frank Cyril *Genesis; the development of hospital libraries in the United Kingdom, including the study of their present and possible future relations with public libraries* (LA thesis) London, LA, 1934.

Periodical articles

Alison, M J H 'Libraries in hospitals' *Book trolley* 3(6), June 1972, 3-10.

Ballandras, M 'IFLA hospital library studies (3): reading in hospitals' *International library review* 6(4), October 1974, 407-409.

Conaway, Sister M C 'Patient/family education: reaching out to well-ness' *Catholic library world* 48, March 1977, 328-331.

Cooper, Brian 'Library services at Rampton hospital' *Health and welfare libraries quarterly* 1(3), September 1974, 46-59.

Cumming, Eileen E 'Children in hospital: do they need a library service?' *Book trolley* 3(3), September 1971, 3-9.

Dragonette, Dorothy B 'The health science library's contribution to patient care' *Bulletin of the Medical Library Association* 61(1), January 1973, 29-32.

Durrant, John 'A library service to geriatric patients in hospitals' *Health and welfare libraries quarterly* 1(4), December 1974, 87-89.

Gardner, Frank M 'IFLA Libraries in Hospitals Sub-section: the integrated hospital library part 2, England' *International library review* 1(1), January 1969, 61-65.

Johnson, B C 'Services an integrated hospital library can and cannot provide' *ALA bulletin* 63(11), December 1969, 1554-1559.

Lewis, M Joy 'Hospital and welfare library services' in Whatley, H A (editor) *British librarianship and information science, 1966-1970* London, LA, 1972, 560-578.

'Library resources for patient education' (Symposium) *AHIL quarterly* 11, winter 1971, 11-15.

Library services in hospitals. Cover title to special issue of *New Zeland library* 38(4), August 1975, 117-232.

Lucioli, Clara E and Baker, Elizabeth M 'IFLA Libraries in Hospital Sub-section: hospital library studies 1967-1971 (8) USA 1967: the role of the public library in hospital library provision' *International library review* 4(3), July 1972, 387-391.

May, Margaret 'The training of volunteers in hospital libraries' in: *Libraries for health and welfare: papers given to the Hospital Libraries and Handicapped Readers Group of Conferences in 1968 and 1969* London, LA, 1971, 34-38.

Paulin, L V 'Libraries in Hospitals Sub-section: hospital library studies 1967-1971 (7) United Kingdom 1971: (b) current developments in hospital libraries *International library review* 4(3), July, 1972, 380-383.

Pemberton, John E 'The role of public library authorities in the de-velopment of hospital library services' *Journal of librarianship* 3(2), April 1971, 101-119.

Scougall, Jean 'Place of the library in the hospital family, outline of the paper presented at the Library Training Institute County Library of Medicine September 14-19, 1969' *AHIL quarterly* 10, spring 1970, 67-72.

Tylor, Dorothy 'Hospital libraries' *The library* 7(83), November 1895, 347-352.

Urch, M E 'Hospital libraries—the past and the present' in: *Libraries for health and welfare: papers given to the Hospital Libraries and Handicapped Readers Group Conferences in 1968 amd 1969* London, LA, 1971, 12-17.

Walsh, Mary A 'Organisation of library services for hospital patients' *UNESCO bulletin for libraries* 23(2), March/April 1969, 77-83.

Yast, Helen 'Standards for library service in institutions: (b) In the health care setting' *Library trends* 21(2), October 1972, 267-285.

PRISON LIBRARIES
Books and pamphlets

American Library Association, Association of Hospital and Institution Libraries: Special Committee on library service to prisoners *Jails need libraries too: guidelines for library service programs to jails* Chicago, ALA, 1974.

Einenkel, J *Intellectual freedom in prisons* Research paper; Albany, State University of New York, 1971.

Gulker, V *Books behind bars* Metuchen (NJ), Scarecrow Press, 1973.

Le Donne, Marjorie E 'Role of the library in a correctional institution' in: *Library and information services for special groups* (editor) Joshua I Smith. New York, Science Associates/International Inc, 1974.

Le Donne, Marjorie E *Survey of library and information problems in correctional institutions, vol I: Findings and recommendations* Arlington (Va), ERIC Document Reproduction Service, ED 095 852, 1974.

MacCormick, Austin H *A brief history of libraries in American correctional institutions* American Correctional Association, Congress of Corrections, 1970, 197-209.

Meffert, L J 'A study of inmate reading habits at Minnesota State Prison' in: *Libraries, readers and book selection* (editor) Jean Spealman Kujoth. Metuchen (NJ), Scarecrow Press, 1969, 137-153.

'Prisons and other correctional institutions' in: Brown, E R *Bibliotherapy and its widening applications* Metuchen (NJ), Scarecrow Press, 1975, 151-179.

Reynolds, R C *Role of librarianship in penal institutions: a historical review and survey of contemporary training programs* Thesis (MA); San José, California State University, 1973.

Rubin, Rhea Joyce *US prison library services and their theoretical base* University of Illinois, Graduate School of Library Science, 1973. (110)

Suvak, Daniel S *Prison inmates' attitudes towards reading and library facilities* Master's research paper submitted to Kent University School of Library Science, 1972.

Werner, O J *Manual for prison law libraries* Rothman/American Association of Law Libraries, 1976.

Periodical articles

Bailey, Andree 'Standards for library service in institutions: (a) In the correctional setting' *Library trends* 21(2), October 1972, 261-266.

Hartz, Frederic R 'Library in the correctional setting: a selected bibliography 1964-1973' *Catholic library world* 46, December 1974, 218-225.

Jeffries, Stephen R 'In case of fire throw this book in!!' *Catholic library world* 46, May-June 1975, 434-437.

Le Donne, Marjorie E 'Summary of court decisions relating to the provision of library services in correctional institutions' *AHIL quarterly* 13, winter/spring 1973, 3-11.

Pearson, A 'Libraries and educational facilities in prisons' *Book trolley* 3(7), September 1972, 3-12.

Poe, Elizabeth Holt 'A spark of hope for prisoners' *Law library journal* 66(1), February 1973, 59-62.

Rubin, Rhea Joyce (editor) 'Breaking-in: library service to prisoners' *Wilson Library bulletin* 51(6), February 1977, 496-533.

Suvak, Daniel 'Federal prison libraries: the quiet collapse' *Library journal* 102(12), June 15 1977, 1341-1344.

Werner, O J 'Present legal status and conditions of prison law libraries' *Law library journal* 66(3), August 1973, 259-271.

Zabel, Jean Marie 'Prison libraries' *Special libraries* 67(1), January 1976, 1-7.

LIBRARY SERVICES FOR THE ELDERLY

American Library Association, Reference and Adult Services Division; Committee on Library Services to an Aging Population *Guidelines for library service to an aging population* RQ14(3), spring 1975, 237-239.

Armour, Jenny 'Library services to the elderly' *Asssistant librarian* 68(10), November 1975, 166-169.

Brooks, Jean 'Older persons and the college-level examination program' *AHIL quarterly* 12, spring/summer 1972, 17-18.

Brothers, Sue C 'Special report: how to start a library when there is no librarian, no room, no books and no budget' *Wilson Library bulletin* 51(2), October 1976, 119-121.

Buswell, Christa H 'Our other customers: reading and the aged' *Wilson Library bulletin* 45(5), January 1971, 467-476.

Casey, Genevieve M 'Public library services to the aging: ASD special report' *American librarian* 2(9), October 1971, 999-1004.

Daffern, Beverley Ann 'Patterns of library service to residents of senior citizens apartment complexes' *AHIL quarterly* 13, summer/fall 1973, 35-43.

Delvalle, June and others 'Reading patterns of the aged in a nursing home environment' by June Delvalle, Dulcy B Miller, and Mary Saldicco in: *Libraries, readers and book selection* (editor) Jean Spealman Kujoth Metuchen (NJ), Scarecrow Press, 1969, 128-132.

Kanner, E E *The impact of gerontological concepts on the principles of librarianship* Thesis (PhD), University of Wisconsin, 1972.

Long, Fern 'The live-long and like it club—the Cleveland public library' *Library trends* 17(1), July 1968, 68-71.

Ludlow, Felicity 'Libraries and the older adult: how well are they served?' *Canadian library journal* 32(1), February 1975, 7-10.

Paparella, Julia B 'Library service for the aging' *Catholic library world* 44, April 1973, 540-544.

Phinney, Eleanor (editor) 'Library services to the aging' *Library trends* 21(3), January 1973, 359-458. (A special issue covering aspects of library service to the elderly.)

Schmidt, L M (editor) 'Library services to the aging' *AHIL quarterly* spring/summer 1972. (Issue devoted to the provision of library facilities for the elderly.)

LIBRARY SERVICES
FOR THE PHYSICALLY DISABLED

Critchley, W E 'Library services for housebound readers in Scotland' *Book trolley* 2(3), September 1968, 54-58.

De Lange, Anna M 'Housebound readers in Sheffield: a survey' *Health and welfare libraries quarterly* 1(2), June 1974, 27-31.

Goldsmith, S 'Library planning for the disabled' *Book trolley* 3(8), December 1972, 3-7.

Kamisar, Hylda and Pollet, Dorothy 'Those missing readers: the visually and physically handicapped' *Catholic library world* 46, May/June 1975, 426-431.

Lewis, M Joy 'Service to housebound readers' *Health and welfare libraries quarterly* 1(2), June 1974, 24-27.

Lucioli, Clara E and Fleak, Dorothy H 'The shut-in—waiting for what?' *ALA bulletin* 58(9), October 1964, 781-784.

Nicholas, Rossley M 'Reading and writing aids for the disabled' *Assistant librarian* 66(3), March 1973, 40-42.

Shaw, Alison 'Writing and reading aids for the physically handicapped' *Journal of librarianship* 4(2), April 1972, 75-90, 97.

Sutton, Johanna G 'Our other customers—shut-ins: consider the confined: methods of reaching-in' *Wilson Library bulletin* 45(5), January 1971, 485-489.

Vasi, John 'Building libraries for the handicapped: a second look' *Journal of academic librarianship* 2(2), May 1976, 82-83.

Velleman, Ruth A 'Library adaptations for the handicapped' *Library journal* 99(18), 15 October 1974, 2713-2716.

Wilson, Barbara L 'Vocational materials: needs assessment—an interim report' *Health and Rehabilitative Library Services Division journal* 2(2), fall 1976, 9-12.

LIBRARY SERVICES FOR THE BLIND
AND VISUALLY HANDICAPPED
Books and pamphlets

American Library Association, Library Administrative Division *Standards for library service for the blind and visually handicapped* Chicago, ALA, 1967.

Cowburn, L M *History and development of the National Library for the Blind* (LA fellowship thesis), 1969.

Emmons, Karen M and Friedman, Morton H 'Development of automated systems at DBPH, Library of Congress' in: *Information revolution: Proceedings of the 38th ASIS annual meeting, vol 12 Boston (Mass) Oct 26-30 1975* (editors) Charles W Husbands and Ruth L Tighe. Washington (DC), American Society for Information Science, 1975, 57-8.

Gill, J M *Orientation maps for the visually handicapped* University of Warwick, 1974.

Library Association and National Association for the Education of the Partially Sighted *Clear print: papers and proceedings of a conference sponsored by the Library Association and the National Association for the Education of the Partially Sighted and held at the Commonwealth Hall, London, on 20th October, 1971* London, LA, 1972 (LA Research publication 9).

Library Association and National Association for the Education of the Partially Sighted *Print for the visually handicapped reader: papers and proceedings of a conference sponsored by the Library Association and the National Association for the Education of the Partially Sighted and held in October 1970.* London, LA (LA research publication 6).

The reading needs of the hard of seeing London, LA, 1974 (LA research publication 13).

Stetten, Kenneth J *Telebook center for the blind. Phase 1 final report* Washington (DC), Mitre Corporation, 1976.

Shaw, Alison *Print for partial sight: a report to the Library Association on books for readers with defective sight* London, LA, 1969.

Periodical articles

Cylke, Frank Kurt 'Free national program to beef up services for the blind and handicapped' *American libraries* 7(7), July/August 1976, 466-7.

'Education of the visually handicapped: the Library Association's memorandum of evidence to the Department of Education and Science . . .' *Book trolley* 2(5), March 1969, 83-92.

Friedman, Morton H 'A comprehensive bibliographical service for the blind and physically handicapped' *Journal of library automation* 8(4), December 1975, 322-335.

Graham, John 'The National Listening Library' *Assistant librarian* 67(7), July 1974, 112-114.

Haycraft, Howard 'Books for the blind: a postscript and an appreciation' *ALA bulletin* 56(9), October 1962, 795-802.

Hunsucker, Coy Kate 'Public library services to blind and physically handicapped children' *Health and Rehabilitative Library Services Division journal* 2(2), fall 1976, 2-5.

Lewis, M Joy 'Large print book publishing' *Library Association record* 73(5), May 1971, 93-94.

Matthews, David 'Blind exposure: some thoughts on book selection' *Book trolley* 3(12), December 1973, 8-12.

Sturt, Ronald 'The talking newspaper' *Book trolley* 2(10), June 1970, 3-12.

Vollans, R F 'Print for the visually handicapped reader: a one day conference' *Library world* 72(846), December 1970, 180-183.

Werner, M M 'Collection development in the Division for the Blind and Physically Handicapped' *Catholic library world* 47, May 1976, 418-419.

LIBRARY SERVICES
FOR THE MENTALLY RETARDED

Bialac, V 'Public library and the retarded patron' *AHIL quarterly* 11, spring 1971, 31-32.

Becker, Mary Justa 'Book power: libraries for the mentally retarded' *AHIL quarterly* 10, spring 1970, 73-74.

Boorer, David 'Do mentally handicapped people need books?' *Book trolley* 3(5), March 1972, 11-13.

Champlin, J L and Champlin, C J 'Telling simple stories with retarded adults' *Catholic library world* 48, March 1977, 322-327.

Clark, D F 'Reading in the mental subnormality hospital' *Book trolley* 3(5), March 1972, 3-8.

Cross, D E *Library materials and services for the emotionally disturbed and brain-injured child* Research paper, Albany, State University of New York, 1971.

Cumming, Eileen E 'Reading for the mentally handicapped: a selective bibliography' *Book trolley* 3(5), March 1972, 14-15.

Gallimore, J E *Criteria for the selection and evaluation of book and non-book materials for mentally retarded adolescents and adults* Thesis (MA), San José, California State University, 1973.

Hannigan, Margaret C 'On the plus side: landmark achievements—standards for library services in resident facilities for the mentally retarded' *AHIL quarterly* 11, spring 1971, 35-38.

Happ, F William 'Multimedia services for retardees in institutions' *Top of the news* 25(3), April 1969, 268-272.

Harris, N G 'Audiovisual resources: resident library services for the mentally retarded' *AHIL quarterly* 11, spring 1971, 35-38.

Hay, Wendy 'Books in care: visiting Lambeth's special care unit' *Assistant librarian* 69(7/8), July/August 1976, 134-135.

Klumb, (Mrs) David and others 'Public library works with the retarded' *AHIL quarterly* 11, spring 1971, 32-34.

Liebig, M 'Direct service to mentally retarded residents in an institution' *AHIL quarterly* 11, spring 1971, 34-35.

Meyer, J R 'Selected bibliography of library services in mental retardation' *AHIL quarterly* 11, spring 1971, 30-31.

Montgomery, Helen 'Special report: outreach to the retarded' *Wilson Library bulletin* 50(9), May 1976, 688-690.

Paton, Xenia 'Teaching the mentally retarded to read: some personal experiences' *Book trolley* 3(5) March 1972, 9-11.

LIBRARY SERVICES FOR THE DEAF

Cory, Patricia B 'Library work with deaf children' *Top of the news* 13(3), March 1957, 33-36.

Da Rold, J and Bray, B 'Service to the deaf' *News notes California Library* 71(1), 1976, 15-20.

Edwards, Fern L 'Individual access to non-print information for deaf students' *Catholic library world* 46, September 1974, 68-70.

Gilbert, Laura Jean 'Materials, program suggestions for hearing-impaired children' *School media quarterly* 4(3), spring 1976, 263-268.

Groff, P 'Childrens' fiction and the psychology of deafness' *School librarian* 24(3), September 1976, 196-202.

Haberer, Isobel J 'Reading and the hard of hearing' *Library Association record* 74(9), September 1972, 162-164.

Hagemeyer, Alice 'Librarian for the deaf' *American libraries* 7(6), June 1976, 354-5.

Limper, Hildak 'Library services to deaf children' *AHIL quarterly* 9(1), fall 1966, 7-10.

Posell, Elsa Z 'Libraries and the deaf patron' *Wilson Library bulletin* 51(5), January 1977, 402-404.

Putnam, Lee 'Information needs of hearing-impaired people' *Health and Rehabilitative Library Services Division journal* 2(1), spring 1976, 2-14.

INDEX

Aberdeen Public Library 114-
115, 126
Adult Training Centres 210
Aged *see* Elderly
AHIL quarterly 77
Akron Summit County Library
Service (Ohio) 215-6
American Bible Society 70
American Correctional Associa-
tion 77, 80
American Federation for the
Blind 172
American Foundation for the
Blind 168, 170, 177, 187
American Library Association
hospital library services 13
hospital library standards
24-5
services to the blind and
partially sighted 167, 170,
182-3, 186
American Library Association.
Adult Education Division.
Committee on Library
Services to an Ageing
Population 100
Committee on Enlarged
Programs for American
Library Service 73
Committee on Institu-
tional Libraries 71-2, 73
Hospital Library Com-
mittee 13
Hospital Library Round
Table 13
American Library Association
and American Correctional
Association.
Joint Committee on prison
libraries 80
American Printing House for the
Blind 167, 172, 174, 177-8, 183
American Prison Association
Committee on Institutional
Libraries 76
American Red Cross 169
Arnold, Martha 154

Ashwell. Correctional Institu-
tion 84
Association of Hospital and
Institutional Libraries (ALA)
see also Health and Rehabilita-
tion Library Services Division
25, 31, 77
Austin Books 185, 190, 192
Austin, Ethel Winifred 155
Aves Report 124

Barbier, Charles 146
Bardon-La Follette Act (1943)
144-5
Battle of the Contractions 147
Battle of the Dots 147
Beveridge Report (1942) 15
Beverley Heights (NJ) Public
Library 207-8
Bibliotherapy 47
Binet, Alfred 198
Birmingham, medical library
network 26
BLAISE 26
Blind
definition of 142-3
reader services 157-164,
171-9
bibliographical aids 158, 173,
175
history
UK 154-6
USA 164-171
see also Braille, Moon,
Talking books
Blind Persons Act (1920) 156
Blue Ribbon Committee on
Correctional Library Services
(California) 78-9
Book trolley 12, 20
Books on record and tape
see Talking books
Boston (Mass) Public Library
110, 165
Braille 128, 145, 146-9, 171,
178
computerised 148-9

227

National Council of Women
21
National Health Service (UK)
15, 16, 17
National Institute for the
Blind 147, 150, 159, 187
see also Royal National
Institute for the Blind
National Library for the Blind
154-8, 172, 185, 192
National Library of Medicine
25
National Listening Library 163
'National Plan for Libraries' 13-14
'Never too late' club. Boston
(Mass) Public Library 110
New Jersey State Library 208
New Portway Reprints large
print series 190
New York
prison association 72
public library 72
state library 72-3, 153
New Zealand Library Association
Hospital Library Service
Committee 21
Nuffield Talking Book Library
151
see also British Talking Book
Service for the Blind

Office of Population Censuses and
Surveys. Social Services Division
121
Old people see Elderly
Older Americans Act 101-2
Optacon 145
Oralism 212
Order of St John see St John
Oregon Education Department
182
Oxford, Medical library network
26

Paget-Gorman sign language 216
Partially sighted
definition 180-2
reading needs 187-90

see also Large print books; Talking
books; Magnification aids
Patients' libraries see Hospital
libraries
Pavilion for the Blind 165-7
Penal systems 83-4
Pentonville Prison 63-4, 66
Philadelphia Free Library 170
Physically handicapped see
Disabled
Poor Law Regulations 16
Pratt-Smoot Bill 168, 169-70
Prince, Jack 186, 187-9
'Print for Partial Sight' 186
Prison Community 83-6
Education programmes 59, 60,
61, 70, 86-9
Prison libraries
finance 60-3
history
UK 58-69
USA 69-80
legal collections 94-5
recreational reading 89-91
staff
professional 58, 62, 64, 66,
67 , 68,69,74, 75,76,95-7
non-professional 61, 62,
68, 74, 75
surveys 58, 63, 64-6, 67,
71-4, 75, 76, 77, 78-9
Public Libraries. Services to
institutions and to groups. See
under subject heading, eg
Hospitals, Prisons, Elderly,
Disabled, etc.
Public Library and Museums
Act, 1964 19, 65

Ravens progressive matrices 199
Recordings for the Blind Inc
New York 172, 174
Red Cross 21
Red Cross Institute for the
Blind (US) 167
Red Cross Library (UK) see
St John and Red Cross Library
Rider, Gertrude T 167-8